Markets In The Firm

A Market-Process Approach to Management

Tyler Cowen

George Mason University

Fairfax, Virginia, USA

and

David Parker

Aston University, Birmingham

Published by The Institute of Economic Affairs

1997

First published in July 1997 by
The Institute of Economic Affairs
2 Lord North Street
Westminster
London SW1P 3LB

Hobart Paper 134
All rights reserved
ISSN 0073-2818
ISBN 0-255 36405-9

Printed in Great Britain by
Hartington Fine Arts Limited, Lancing, West Sussex
Set in Baskerville Roman 11 on 12 point

Contents

FOREWORD

Since Ronald Coase, in a famous 1937 article, questioned why firms exist economists have debated why some resources are allocated in markets whereas others are allocated in firms. Are there fundamental differences between the two so that firms must inevitably remain centres of 'command-and-control' even within market systems? Professors Tyler Cowen and David Parker think not: firms can benefit from using market principles to allocate resources within their organisations.

In Hobart Paper 134, they consider some of the implications for management of different views of the firm. They point to the need, in these days of global markets and increased uncertainty, for firms to be flexible and responsive to market-place requirements. By contrast, from about the 1920s until the 1960s, world markets were dominated by European and United States' businesses and there was more tariff and quota protection of individual markets than exists today: consequently Western firms faced less intensely competitive markets than they do now. It was the heyday of command-and-control methods and centralised strategic planning. The 'scientific management' principles of Frederick Winslow Taylor – which emphasised 'top-down' planning in the firm – were still very influential. Similarly, in macro-economic affairs, belief in planning lingered.

However, according to Cowen and Parker, just as central economic planning has broken down so planning at the level of the firm is proving inadequate. 'Taylorist' methods, though they continue in some firms, are demonstrably too rigid as the environment becomes less stable. Led by Japanese companies, many firms have adopted new decentralised and flexible management structures in which, for example, employees come together in teams for specific purposes. There is more scope for individual initiative and quicker decision-making: successful companies require a high proportion of skilled and know-ledgeable workers, just as they did in the days of craft production.

The danger in less formally structured types of organisation is, of course, that anarchy will reign. As the authors put it:

'...how can the need for overall control to prevent anarchy be combined with the degree of flexibility necessary to adapt to changes in the external environment?' (page 32)

The dilemma can be resolved, in their view, by drawing ideas from recent developments in theories of the firm – in particular, the 'contracts' view which stresses similarities between resource allocation in markets and in firms because in both cases the principal issues are incentives and motivation. Successful firms will be those which are able to '...mimic markets in discovering and mobilising dispersed information.'(page 78)

Some companies are well along the road to applying market principles to management. Cowen and Parker give, as a leading example, a US oil company, Koch Industries Inc. in Wichita, Kansas, whose success seems attributable partly to its whole-hearted embrace of market principles. In Section IV they explain the factors which appear to have led to success in Koch Industries, including continuously refined mission statements, profit centres, a flexible organisational structure in which teams cut across traditional functions and a system of incentives based on the discovery of knowledge.

In their Conclusions (Section V), the authors point to the paradox that in market economies, '... large quantities of resources are allocated outside the market and within organisations.'(page 74) As they also explain, since the days when Alfred Marshall was writing about the economics of business, mainstream economists have neglected the study of the firm – principally because of the influence of the perfect competition paradigm in which the firm has only an insignificant place. Other disciplines (organisation theory and strategic management, for instance) have filled the vacuum left by this neglect. Cowen and Parker argue that economists should re-discover the use of micro-economics in business if they wish to make their subject relevant again. Otherwise some of its most interesting areas will continue to be captured by researchers and teachers in other disciplines.

The main conclusion reached by Professors Cowen and Parker – that market principles are appropriate guides in business decisions as well as providing the best structure for economy-wide resource allocation – are intuitively appealing and they provide considerable evidence both from the academic literature and from practical observation of firms to support their case. However, as always in Institute publications, the

6

conclusions are those of the authors not of the IEA (which has no corporate view), its Trustees, Advisers or Directors. Hobart Paper 134 is published as a stimulating discussion which carries into new territory the debate about the relative advantages of centralised planning and markets.

July 1997   COLIN ROBINSON
Editorial Director, The Institute of Economic Affairs
Professor of Economics, University of Surrey

THE AUTHORS

Tyler Cowen received his PhD in economics from Harvard University in 1987, and is currently Professor of Economics at George Mason University. His books include *Public Goods and Market Failures: Explorations in the New Monetary Economics* (co-authored with Randall Kroszner), and the forthcoming *In Praise of Commercial Culture*, under contract to Harvard University Press. He has also published a wide variety of articles in micro-economics, rational choice ethics and public economics, and he is working on a book on the economics of fame and approbation.

David Parker, PhD, is Professor of Business Economics and Strategy at the Aston University Business School in Birmingham. He received his doctorate from the Cranfield School of Management. He has lectured in a number of UK universities and was a visiting senior researcher at the University of York and the University of Naples. He has contributed widely to journals and books on economics and management. Recent books include *The Essence of the Economy*, (second edition 1996) and *The Essence of Business Economics*, (second edition 1997), both published by Prentice Hall; *Profit and Enterprise: The Political Economy of Profit* (1991), published by Harvester Wheatsheaf; and *The Impact of Privatisation* (1997), published by Routledge. He is also co-author (with R. Stacey) of *Chaos, Management and Economics: the Implications of Non-Linear Thinking*, IEA Hobart Paper 125 (1994).

ACKNOWLEDGEMENTS

We thank Penelope Brook Cowen, Jerome R. Ellig, Richard H. Fink, Wayne E. Gable, Charles G. Koch, John C. Pittenger and two anonymous referees for useful comments and suggestions. The Center for Market Processes, George Mason University, provided financial assistance to Tyler Cowen.

I. INTRODUCTION

'Whoever desires constant success must change his conduct with the times.' Niccolo Machiavelli, 1469-1527

Businesses around the world face increasing turbulence in their economic and social environments. The pace of change in market economies seems to be ever accelerating. In consequence, it has become something of a cliché to say that competitive advantage now lies with the 'learning organisation' – an organisation which constantly monitors its external environment, learns, adapts, and responds speedily to change (Burgoyne, 1992). In today's world, information or knowledge – not labour or capital as formerly – is becoming the critical factor of production for many organisations (Drucker, 1993; Leonard-Barton, 1995).

Competitive advantage depends upon an organisation's ability to monitor its external environment, sense the need for change and respond appropriately before competitors outpace it. The firm must be market-oriented and flexible with the ability to generate and integrate information. It requires an internal structure and systems that can process knowledge and information from the external boundaries of the firm and produce appropriate internal responses. The purpose of this *Hobart Paper* is to illustrate how an attention to market principles *within* the firm can improve the ability of organisations to learn and adapt.

Since the Industrial Revolution firms have grown and developed largely on a functional basis. Some departments have been concerned directly with the consumer or suppliers (for example, marketing or procurement), whereas others have provided internal services across the organisation (for instance, finance, information technology (IT) and personnel). Alfred Sloan introduced a structure suitable for such functionalism at General Motors in the 1920s.[1] Sloan believed that managers should determine the company's

---

[1] Another architect of the modern, hierarchical corporation was Henry Ford; hence the term 'Fordism' is sometimes applied to this structure.

strategy, design its structure and select its control systems. It should be controlled from top down through a functional structure forming a classic management hierarchy or a pyramid of control. Senior management should be firmly in control of strategy and operations; to this end information flows would be mainly up and down the organisation. The senior managers would plan and control their businesses in a fashion similar to the way Soviet commissars from the 1920s planned and controlled their empires. Lower down the organisation, local management would run the separate plants and be responsible, in the main, for operational matters.

Heyday of 'Command and Control'

Modern corporations, with their emphasis on 'command and control', are planning systems and when companies become too large to be controlled effectively by one management layer, they are divided into divisions and sub-divisions. Nevertheless, overall control of business strategy is still maintained by 'top management' or what may be called the 'strategy makers'. It is significant that the heyday of this monolithic, planned corporation was from the 1920s to the 1970s, a time when US and European businesses dominated world markets aided by cartels, oligopolistic market structures, tariffs, and a relative paucity of global competition. It was also a time when 'economic planning' became fashionable at the macro-economic level.

As competitive pressures rose in North America and Western Europe from the 1960s, however, change became inevitable. At first managers (supported by management theorists and consultants) attempted to refine the control process and structure. They developed such innovations as 'management by objectives' and favoured matrix forms of organisational structure.[2] Rarely was the entire notion of command, control and centralised strategic planning questioned.

Today, however, the Sloan corporation is in retreat. It has proved too expensive in terms of administration costs and too

---

[2] The matrix form is a combination of structures often taking the form of product and geographical divisions or functional and divisional structures operating together; see Johnson and Scholes (1997, pp. 373-76), and the discussion on pages 50-51 below.

slow and inflexible to adapt to rapid market changes. Some successful companies (for example, Canon, Intel, 3M and ABB) have moved away from the idea that top managers have a monopoly of wisdom and that the workforce is there to put that wisdom into practice. In large hierarchical firms, structured around specialist functions, the bulk of the firm's employees often had little direct contact with external consumers and the market-place. In these organisations growth occurred to the point where there were few effective connections between the organisation and the market-place and employees could not easily see a direct relationship between the firm's performance in the market and their salaries and employment. It is not surprising, therefore, that competitive advantage was lost. A successful organisation needs a constant flow of market signals *throughout* and not just up and down the organisation to enable appropriate responses. Denied this flow of information the firm ceases to learn or, at least, learning occurs slowly or in fits and starts.

Organisations that lose their ability to undertake a constant two-way flow of communication with their markets are likely to be those that lose their competitive standing. Contrary to common opinion, even among managers, the world is not dominated by a set number of giant transnational companies which have some kind of economic immortality. Even the largest companies prove vulnerable to competitive forces (including take-overs). For example, of the top 50 companies in the UK in 1984, around 20 per cent have now disappeared. Of the list in 1965 about half have gone. Of the 30 firms that made up the original *Financial Times* Ordinary Share Index in 1935 only nine – Associated Portland Cement (now Blue Circle), Bass, Courtaulds, GEC, GKN, ICI, Tate and Lyle, Turner and Newall, and Vickers – survive in a similar form and even in these cases there has been considerable restructuring over the years. In the United States the record is similar. Although 16 of the 30 firms in the Dow Jones index in 1935 are still in the index today, only one company in the 1900 index still survives – General Electric. Almost 40 per cent of the Fortune 500 companies listed in 1983 have since passed on (Caulkin, 1995).

Yet some companies survive much longer – for example, Cambridge University Press goes back to 1534, Mitsui and Sumitomo in Japan date from the 17th and 18th centuries and

11

Du Pont from 1801. Longevity appears to result from complex factors involving internal management and its appreciation of and responses to external threats and opportunities, perhaps coupled with an element of good fortune. Successful organisations create and maintain an ability to process information about their external environment and to change.

Information as a factor of production is making old functional structures and methods of organisation and planning redundant in many areas of business. The successful use of knowledge involves not only its generation, but also its mobilisation and integration, requiring a change in the way it is handled and processed. For example, treating quality problems as the exclusive purview of specialist departments slows down and can even distort the information flow, thereby damaging the quality of service to the consumer.

To increase knowledge and speed up its diffusion, companies are 'delayering', leading to the loss of large numbers of jobs, especially for middle managers. In more traditionally structured companies, middle managers largely act as information go-betweens in the management hierarchy, passing and codifying information between senior management and the workforce. By contrast, in new 'flatter' companies workers are empowered to take more management-type decisions without upward reference. The need for information go-betweens is removed and the number of 'job classifications' is reduced. For example, when General Motors brought in Toyota to help it run the Fremont auto manufacturing plant, the number of job classifications dropped from 82 to three relatively flexible categories.[3]

Emergence of Team Working

In parallel with the loss of hierarchical and functional structures is the rise of team working. Teams of workers are given the power to be largely self-functioning, tackling production and strategic decisions. Sometimes teams will come together from various parts of the company for a particular project and, once that project is completed, disband. Firms also contract out more services to gain flexibility and drive down cost, but these contracts are not necessarily based on short-term competitive tendering. Many

---

[3]   See Ingrassia and White (1994, p.52).

businesses have reduced their numbers of recognised suppliers and entered into various forms of 'partnership sourcing' under which suppliers and the main contracting firms retain their independence while building long-term collaboration in production and product development. In the last 15 years, for instance, Rover cars in Britain has reduced its number of suppliers from around 2,000 to 700 with a core of 350 now accounting for over 80 per cent of spending.

All these developments share a common theme – the growing dominance of knowledge and informational considerations in competitive advantage and the related need for flexibility and speedy reaction to market changes. But this essential agility poses a major challenge for organisations, namely how to attain the desired looser and flatter organisational form without creating a breakdown of decision-making. There are obvious dangers in too many people, teams or divisions 'doing their own thing'. Firms may tear themselves apart as groups head off in separate directions. Costly pet projects may quickly haemorrhage the firm's financial resources. The loss of middle-manager posts risks the creation of a power gulf between newly empowered staff and senior management or strategic decision-makers. Contracting out for supplies risks the loss of important in-house skills that in the future may be fundamental to the firm's competitive advantage and long-term survival. How can management hold together such a confederate structure, encouraging local flexibility and responsiveness to the market-place without losing control altogether?

In this *Hobart Paper* we suggest the beginnings of an answer to these questions. We consider how the principles of resource allocation in the 'external' market-place can be applied to resource allocation 'within the firm'. These two seemingly different types of resource allocation problems share considerable similarities. We show how firms can exploit the advantages of market exchange to improve business profitability. Firms must institute appropriate safeguards to ensure the accumulation of knowledge and its successful processing, translating it into the actions of their members. In a similar way, markets involve the bringing together and successful co-ordination of the knowledge and actions of all participants.

Our approach to organisational economics brings together several strands of economic thought. In the economics literature, some economists have already recognised a blurred distinction between firms and markets (for example, Richardson, 1960 and 1972; Cheung, 1983; Fama, 1980; Simon, 1991).[4] We build on their insights and apply our approach to the particular problems of management. In particular, we draw on the Coasian analysis of the firm as developed in the modern economics literature on contracts and business organisation (Coase, 1937, 1991), including formal models to analyse how contracts and property rights influence business outcomes. Economists from both the Chicago School and the 'New' institutionalist approach to industrial organisation have developed a powerful view of 'markets and hierarchies' that we exploit.[5]

The Market Process Approach

Our approach complements the market process or 'Austrian' school of economics which analyses the market as a dynamic process of both co-operation and competition, rather than as comparative states of equilibrium as emphasised in much neo-classical theorising. The market process view of economics has been shaped particularly by Carl Menger, Ludwig von Mises, Friedrich Hayek and Israel Kirzner (Kirzner, 1997). Our approach also complements the fast-expanding strategic management literature, less well-known to many economists, which is primarily concerned with the capability of firms to compete and gain competitive advantage.[6] The study of strategic management has displaced economics at many business schools around the world, a development on which we comment later in this study.

At least three views of the conceptual differences and similarities between firms and markets can be found in the litera-

---

[4] Simon correctly recognises that the modern market economy is an organisational economy.

[5] A recent text by Milgrom and Roberts (1992), introduces the literature superbly. Another useful source is Ricketts (1994). Applications of contemporary economics to business strategy can be found in the new *Journal of Economics and Management Strategy*, published by the MIT Press.

[6] Peter Senge (1993) offers some of the best of strategic management theory. Johnson and Scholes (1997) provide a useful overview of the subject.

ture, although they are not always fully articulated. According to the first view, firms and markets are simply two different names for the same set of phenomena. Each 'firm' activity involves a contractual market transaction. The world consists of collections of owned resources – which we call firms – and trades of those resources – which we call markets. Firms and markets are two sides of the same coin, rather than substitute means of organising production. This view does not require any particular claims about how production is organised.[7] While this first view offers a potentially useful focus for analysis, we use the terms firm and market in accord with a second and different sense.

In this approach firms and markets are not exactly the same, but rather they differ in empirical terms. They refer to different means of organising economic activity, albeit means that *do not differ substantially in kind.* In particular, market transactions are usually relatively short term, impersonal, and characterised by clearly defined exchanges. A classic example of market activity occurs when we buy milk from a supermarket. By contrast, firms typically involve longer and more complex contracts, usually with recurring interaction under the guise of an ongoing formal relationship. A classic kind of firm activity arises when a manager directs a worker regarding his or her day-to-day duties.

This second view does not seek to find a clear-cut distinction between firms and markets. Rather the difference between the firm and the market as a resource allocator involves what might more usefully be viewed as subtle differences relating to the form of contracting. We will argue, in particular, that firms can draw upon some of the efficiency advantages of markets without losing the traditional organisational advantages of the business enterprise.

The third view, which we reject, suggests that firms and markets differ fundamentally in kind. Typically, firms are seen as similar to planned economies rather than to markets. Ronald Coase in his seminal article on 'The Nature of the Firm' in 1937 cited approvingly D.H. Robertson who described the position of firms in market economies as 'islands of conscious power in the ocean of unconscious co-operation like

---

7   Cheung (1983), for instance, appears to adopt this view in our reading of him.

lumps of butter coagulating in a pail of buttermilk'.[8] The major problem for these islands of conscious power is making and taking centralised decisions in a way that ensures competitive success. We consider, and criticise, this view in more detail in Section III. In addition to some theoretical problems considered later on, we view Robertson's conceptualisation as over-emphasising the differences between firms and markets.[9] In our view, firms should be trying to exploit the advantages of markets, rather than running themselves as mini-command economies. If managers try to act like central planners, their firms will usually fail eventually for the same reasons that central planning failed in Central and Eastern Europe.

Hayek implicitly suggested a fruitful approach to management issues when he wrote:

'The real central problem of economics as a social science...is how the spontaneous interaction of a number of people, each possessing only bits of knowledge, brings about a state of affairs...which could be brought about by deliberate direction only by somebody who possesses the combined knowledge of all these individuals.' (Hayek, 1948, p.79.)

Hayek addressed his comments towards economic planning at the macro-economic level, but the same point applies at the micro-economic level as well. A comprehensive approach to resource allocation must embrace the creation, assimilation, and transmission of information about resource demand and supply *within* firms as well as within markets. To restate Hayek's nostrum in terms of our view of the firms-markets distinction as set out in this *Hobart Paper*:

The real central problem of management is how the spontaneous interaction of people within the firm, each possessing only bits of knowledge, can bring about the competitive success that could only be brought about by the deliberate direction of a senior management that possesses the combined knowledge of all of its employees and contractors.

---

8   Coase (1937, p. 388).

9   Coase did state in his 1937 paper that there could be no hard and fast line between the firm and the market but he did not develop this view.

The view of management as central planners lies behind much management thought and practice in this century. Here we identify how the loosely-coupled firm can use the principles of market economics to retain constructive learning while avoiding instability and breakdown. Our approach to the market and organisations has been influenced by the management philosophy of W. Edwards Deming (Deming, 1982, 1988). Deming had a philosophy of management based on learning in which the success of a business lay in constant improvement, using the contributions of everybody working in it. He emphasised the importance of co-operation within the firm, civil treatment of employees, and the rôle of self-esteem in fostering productive activity.

Although Deming operated outside the management mainstream for much of the post-war period, today he has an avid following among leading business managers, especially in the United States and Japan. Deming contributed greatly to the Japanese style of production that has proved so effective since the 1950s, especially with regard to statistical quality control and the mobilisation of information within the firm. In contrast to mainstream strategic management and the Deming approach, however, we lay greater stress on the explicit application of market-based economic theory to managerial problems.[10]

Using Market Mechanisms in the Firm

Our study complements market process or Austrian economics from an organisational perspective. We argue that firms should rely on market-based mechanisms to an increasing degree, and that the problems of command approaches to management resemble the problems faced by all forms of central planning of resource allocation.[11] We contend that market mechanisms are not used within firms to their full potential, or anything near that potential. The problems that many firms experience are because of their inability to mobilise successfully market incentives and market means of generating, processing and integrating knowledge. The price mechanism has proved itself over the last two centuries to be a highly efficient way of transmitting and processing inform-

---

[10] For an introduction to Deming's management philosophy, see Mann (1989). On the nature of Japanese production see Womack, Jones and Ross (1990).

[11] Gable and Ellig (1993) and Cowen and Ellig (1995).

17

ation from diverse sources without the heavy hand of central planning.

This *Hobart Paper* is structured as follows. In Section II we look at how the nature of production and therefore management have changed since the Industrial Revolution and, in particular, we emphasise how advances in information technology make it possible and necessary to combine the advantages of mass production and organisational flexibility. In Section III we return to the nature of the firm and the literature on markets and hierarchies and begin to see how the principles of market economics can be applied in assessing the similarities of firm and market transactions. In Section IV details of some particular applications of market economics to the firm are provided. Section V includes some observations on the direction of economics, as well as a summary of the main arguments of our study and the conclusions.

II. THE CHANGING NATURE OF PRODUCTION

Management is concerned with the acquisition, control and allocation of resources within organisations. The firm brings together capital inputs from shareholders and loan creditors, the workforce as a provider of labour services, and raw materials and components from other suppliers. The firm is therefore a forum for joint production of outputs in which management determines and co-ordinates the various inputs to achieve competitive advantage. To the extent that the resulting joint production is efficiently undertaken to meet the needs of consumers, profits result: shareholders, workers, suppliers and management therefore prosper.

At one level, therefore, nothing much has changed in production over the last few hundred years. The firm today is much like a firm a few centuries ago even though the scale of production, the form of organisation and the technology used have altered dramatically. From another viewpoint, however, there have been noticeable and important changes in the contracting for inputs and the incentives of those working in the firm. Unlike some earlier forms of economic activity, notably serfdom and slavery, capitalism (which developed from the late middle ages) involves voluntary contracting. Economic pressures may induce an input supplier to accept an offer of employment, but such pressure is far removed from the coercion experienced under serfdom or slavery. Under capitalism suppliers of labour, capital and materials usually supply in relatively competitive markets with a choice of purchasers. Although the advantages of competitive private markets for consumers are well known, there are parallel advantages for input suppliers. The competitive market-place enhances the welfare of input suppliers over time by bidding up their returns.

To understand how management is changing today, it is useful to review how production has changed over the two centuries or so since the beginning of the Industrial Revolution. The history of production management can be divided into certain stages of production defined or described by the

Figure 1: Stages of Production

Earliest Times-Late 18th century	Late 18th-mid-19th century	Late 19th-early 20th century	1920s-1960s	1970s-1980s	1990s	Post '2000'
Craft Production	Early Factories	Beginnings of Mass Production	Taylorism	Early Computer-isation	CIM/CAD*	?

* CIM = Computer integrated manufacturing
CAD = Computer aided design
Together they involve the central use of computing power in the manufacture of a product from initial design to production.

20

predominant technologies used (Figure 1).[1] Each stage implies an appropriate orientation of the firm to features of its external environment, such as market size, consumer sophistication, international trade patterns and factor endowments.

The pace of change in industry has accelerated as the external environment facing firms has changed ever more rapidly. Even taking a short time-frame, the rate of change appears much faster now in many industries than it was as little as 30 years ago. In consequence, methods of working and management thinking are having to be more frequently reassessed. Products and even processes of production seem to become obsolete more quickly than before. It is not surprising, therefore, that management life now appears unpredictable and chaotic (Peters, 1987; Parker and Stacey, 1994).

Craft Production

Craft production was the earliest stage of production, lasting for thousands of years. It was swept away in many, though by no means all, industries during the Industrial Revolution. Its feature is reliance on handicraft techniques. The skilled craftsman uses hand tools to make what are essentially individual products. Each product may be designed and produced to meet a specific purchaser's requirements. For example, a farmer might ask for the supply of a plough adapted to the particular needs of his soil. In this type of production no two items produced need be exactly the same. Also, the craftsman might alter his tasks, for example producing a spade one day and a harness the next. Craft production was inherently flexible in terms of both outputs and production processes.

The attainment of quality, one of the major concerns in modern production, was incorporated into craft production. Because the craftsman traded on his reputation, usually within a localised market-place, there was an inbuilt incentive to achieve and maintain high-quality production. Craft prod-

---

[1] The following account benefited from discussion with Stephen Howard of AMTEK Ltd. and we acknowledge his contribution to the formulation of some of the ideas in this section.

uction, however, had two obvious disadvantages: first, it ruled out any substantial economies of scale and limited the degree of division of labour leading to specialisation. Second, the high variety in production implied low precision and limited standardisation in manufacture. Therefore parts were rarely interchangeable.

Craft production was gradually replaced in many areas of manufacture from the 18th century as mass markets and mass production methods developed.

Early Factory Systems

The introduction of factory production is associated with the mid-18th century Industrial Revolution. Though the machines used were crude by modern standards, in Britain they changed centuries of manufacturing methods, particularly when they were coupled with the new steam power. In textiles, spinning and weaving machines and in engineering simple lathes and drills resulted in large gains in productivity, while the need for factories to house the new machines led to the decline of domestic or cottage production. As the number of individuals employed within the organisation rose, more specialisation of tasks evolved. Craft skills declined, though craftsmen were still used in the design of the new machines and in activities still relatively unaffected by the new methods, such as the cutlery trade.

The Beginnings of Mass Production

Early factories were still relatively small-scale operations by modern standards. But, as early as the turn of the 19th century, the nature of 20th-century manufacturing was being shaped in the United States. In New Haven, Connecticut, Eli Whitney introduced early mass production methods into the machining of gun parts. Traditionally, each gun had been produced individually with its own barrel, stock and other parts, even when produced to a common design.

Whitney revolutionised the manufacture of guns by achieving sufficient accuracy in manufacture that gun parts became interchangeable. As precise machining lathes evolved, the introduction of standardisation in manufacture spread gradually to other forms of mechanical production. By the end of the 19th century, the Singer company in the United States had taken the process a step further by perfecting factory techniques to produce large volumes of sewing machines. It was this resulting 'mass production', combining standardisation of parts and large production runs, that formed the basis for the success of American industry in world markets in the first half of the 20th century.

Taylorist Mass Production

Mass production involves scaling up manufacturing to deliver both volume and reduction in unit cost. The result is repetitive production, usually on a batch basis. Such large-scale manufacture required new types of companies and new forms of working. Highly specialised manufacturing machinery reduced the need for craft skills and increased the demand for unskilled and semi-skilled factory operatives. In effect, labour in 'Taylorist' plants (see below) became as homogeneous and interchangeable as the outputs produced. A clear division between staff functionaries who planned and supervised the work (salaried, 'white collar' staff) and the production or line workers (waged, 'blue collar' workers) developed. Productivity rose although product variety in some respects declined. Organisational structures became deep, functional and highly specialised. Quality was not built into the production process but instead had to be controlled by monitoring. A proportion of defects was accepted as inevitable.

During the 20th century, mass production and the associated organisation of labour were encapsulated in the notion of 'scientific management' which endorsed the separation of 'thinkers' (management) from 'doers' (labour). Consumers became richer and manufacturers attempted to respond to growing market demand through product differentiation, even if it was only in terms of minor styling changes. More complex multi-line factories and multi-plant companies resulted.

Two writers were particularly important in shaping thinking on the best form of organisation under mass production. The first was Max Weber (1864-1920) and the second was Frederick W. Taylor (1856-1915).

Today the word 'bureaucracy' has a distinctly negative connotation. The German economist and sociologist Max Weber, however, considered bureaucracy the ideal institution for large organisations. He saw it as the most efficient, perhaps the only way to control a large and complex organisation. In Weber's analysis, real authority lies in the 'rules' which provide the basis for organisational stability by limiting the power of the 'officials'. Weber's bureaucracy was a well-oiled machine.

'The authority to give the commands required for the discharge of (the assigned) duties should be exercised in a stable way. It is strictly delimited by rules concerning the coercive means... which may be placed at the disposal of officials.' (Weber, 1948, p.650.)

Frederick Winslow Taylor began his career as a worker in industry before becoming an engineer and later one of the first management gurus. Whereas Weber was primarily concerned with the subjects of authority and control, Taylor was interested in efficiency. To achieve higher efficiency, he advocated a form of 'scientific management' in which specialism or division of labour would dominate. He proposed that the task of first-line management be split into eight specialisms, each the responsibility of a separate manager. The firm as a vertical hierarchy with functional specialisms – such as finance, sales and personnel – became the norm. Tasks both on the production line and in the offices were rigidly defined.

The main hallmarks of scientific management are the division between 'staff' and 'line'. Taylor viewed the line worker as essentially dumb and capable of only repetitive, directed tasks, writing:

'Now one of the very first requirements for a man who is fit to handle pig iron as a regular occupation is that he shall be so stupid and so phlegmatic that he more nearly resembles in his mental make-up the ox than any other type.'[2]

His belief was that workers are less efficient if they are allowed discretion, initiative or spontaneity. Under 'scientific management' in the expanding corporations the proportion of administrators and managers to production workers grew, as did top-down managerial control.

The scientific best way of doing the job was to be identified by management and imposed on workers. Taylor wrote: 'All possible brain work should be removed from the shop and

---

[2] The quotation is from Taylor (1911, p.59).

centred in the planning or buying-out department'. It was the clear rôle of management to define tasks, change work, evaluate and reward performance, and hire and fire. In addition, in an attempt to reduce uncertainty, a number of firms established influential corporate planning departments whose job it was to anticipate future production needs.[3]

Workers at the lowest levels were permitted little or no discretion over production. They were trained in limited skills for the precise task they were allocated on the production line. In an organisation where people are treated as 'labour units', worker alienation and unionisation grow: in time this worker alienation coupled with unionisation became an important barrier to further productivity growth.

The weaknesses of Taylorism lay in its underlying rationale: large-scale, de-personalised production to achieve economies of scale in manufacture. The pyramid or hierarchical command structure inevitably slowed down decision-making and exacerbated latent hostility between workers and management.[4] In the heyday of this production method – from the 1920s to the 1960s – it proved best at coping with a relatively stable external environment. Hierarchical production with its inevitable rules and procedures (the 'rule book') implied forms of production that needed infrequent change. Scientific management has proved much less well adapted to the faster pace of change in world markets today.

The End of Taylorism

Scientific management lives on in many companies. But as market demand has become more varied and dynamic, it has caused havoc with the steady-state production methods to which Taylorism is best suited. Moreover, the success of Japan in world markets has been associated with a rejection of Taylorist methods. As Kanosuke Matsushita, a leading Japanese industrialist, commented, contrasting Japanese with European and US industry (1988, p.15): 'Yes, we will win and

---

[3] On the link between planning and scientific management see H.S. Person (1929, pp.15-16). Central control and planning were intrinsic to Taylorism. Interestingly, both Lenin and Trotsky were quite taken by Taylor's 'scientific management' (Boettke, 1990) and indeed, one can say they built a society on it with disastrous consequences.

[4] The organisational pyramid involved command control, spans of responsibility and tiered levels of authority.

you will lose. For you are not able to rid your minds of the obsolete Taylorism that we never had.'

Rich consumers have demanded more individuality as well as higher quality in the outputs produced. One response from the 1960s was the beginnings of the 'quality movement'. At first this took the form of inspecting out more defects by increasing the number of inspections. This, however, added to production overheads and therefore increased costs. In the face of growing competition from Japan, European and American companies have had to try to build in quality without losing economies of scale. The period from the 1960s was associated with a movement to quality engineering and business control using new computer technology.

At the same time, increasing competition led to more dynamism and uncertainty in markets and so firms turned to producing more models to raise the odds of achieving a winner in the market-place. The combination of a more dynamic market and the need to raise quality, however, challenges the achievement of variety, economies of scale and consumer satisfaction. Centralised and hierarchical management systems have been undermined. A simplified company is required with much faster response rates to changes in the market-place.

Computerisation was central to the new forms of manufacturing organisation that developed from the 1960s. Numerically controlled machines enabled leading-edge companies to achieve the versatility of general purpose tooling (non-specialist production) with the productivity of dedicated (specialist production) machines. Different operations could be combined on single machines, permitting more flexibility in production in the form of shorter production runs and more varied outputs. At the same time, the accuracy of the machines enabled quality to be built into the production process. Later, computer integrated manufacturing took the use of computers a logical stage further by basing the whole production process on the advanced technology.

Under Taylorism the product is designed by a design department and then production engineers convert the design into a product for the market. Eventually the marketing department and sales force see the new product and begin to formulate a sales campaign. The result generally is a long period between conception of a new product and its entry into the market. Ross Perot is well known for his observation that it takes General Motors five years to introduce a new product, while it took the United States less than four years to fight and win the Second World War (Badaracco, 1987)! Computer integrated manufacturing (CIM) coupled with computer aided design (CAD) permit design, production and marketing to work together to speed up the entry of a new product into the market and to get quality right first time. Once the design is agreed, it can be transmitted directly from the computer to the assembly-line machines.

CAD is also a communication technology which allows for more co-operative links between firms and their suppliers. Business units are best viewed not as single entities but instead as integral parts of a complex production or *value chain* (Porter, 1985). In certain circumstances this modern approach to production places a premium on more collaboration and less competition between firms and suppliers, perhaps leading to the use of fewer, favoured suppliers who can achieve guaranteed quality and rapid delivery times.[5]

With computerisation, the organisation of manufacturing is changing just as it changed with the Industrial Revolution and the onset of mass production. Businesses are moving decision-making closer to the production line and to the consumer, thereby leading to localised production units with a high degree of operating autonomy. Production is being organised in cells or teams including highly trained personnel. The boundary between the firm and its suppliers is becoming more blurred. The next step will be to integrate whole value chains by building computer-linked relationships between consumers and suppliers. The link with the customer becomes necessary because the market is increasingly turbulent and requires more sensitive marketing to assess consumer demands. Retail

---

[5] The emphasis on 'lean supply' and 'lean processes' has led to useful consideration of value added at each chain of the production process. Lean supply involves continuous improvement with devolved power to shop-floor teams linked along the process flow. Each chain of the operation must add value. From this has come the notion of reduced competition and more collaboration between firms and their suppliers and 'partnership sourcing' using a reduced number of preferred suppliers. However, the emphasis on collaboration may be leading to a misunderstanding of the nature of competition and market exchange, which occurs where there is the scope for mutual gain; see Parker and Hartley (1996).

stores are now playing a part in this development by relaying details of consumers' purchases by computer directly to the manufacturers, who can then adapt production immediately.

Adapting quickly to consumer needs is now a key source of competitive advantage. But in addition, computerised technology permits more decision-taking at the line level. The nature of the workforce therefore changes. Far fewer but much more highly educated and trained personnel are required. Workers must now be thinkers rather than simply doers as under Taylorism (Sampson, 1995). One consequence is a decline in worker alienation and in unionisation. Although fewer workers are needed at both staff and line levels within modern factories, those workers who do remain have the potential for enhanced status, higher wages, and greater opportunities for job satisfaction and individual advancement.

Implications for Business Organisation

Today growing international competition places major demands on manufacturing regarding variety of output, quality and speed to the market. Market changes are moving manufacturing farther and farther away from steady-state, low variety, long-batch production runs, relevant to Taylorist methods, to high variety and smaller runs. Quality is now a *pre-requisite* to remain in the market.

Organisations are adopting new forms of decentralisation to cope with the instability, uncertainty and pace of change of the market-place, as summarised under the heading of 'Leading Edge Firms' (see Box, p. 29) (Kanter, 1990; Bartlett and Ghoshal, 1989 and 1990; Tiernan, 1993). In cluster or network working, employees of undifferentiated rank may operate temporarily on a certain task or tasks in teams. The clusters are largely autonomous and engage in decentralised decision-making and planning (Drucker, 1992; Tiernan, 1993, p.60). Clusters do away with much of the organisational hierarchy and economise on administration and management costs. They are conducive to individual initiative ('intrapreneurship') and faster decision-taking. They facilitate organisational flexibility; but they also have dangers, in particular a loss of management control, a loss of organisational direction, and wasteful duplication.

28

Leading Edge Firms

Changes
- flatter structures (delayering)
- less bureaucracy
- end of the management pyramid
- end of scientific management
- wider spans of control
- divisionalisation/dismemberment
- cross-functional team working, clusters, networks
- less formality
- joint ventures and collaboration
- managing the firm as an organism not a machine

Threats
- more difficulty in remaining in control – excessive instability
- lack of organisational coherence
- information overload.

Few organisations have yet adopted the cluster form of production fully even though it has been advocated as 'leading edge'. The reorganisation required seems too great and senior management rightly fears the consequences of lack of control since they have to account for performance to their shareholders. Nevertheless, in the US Rank Xerox, Du Pont and General Electric are experimenting with cluster-type structures and in the UK British Petroleum is now structured around 16 clusters supported by three functional areas: Business Services, Engineering Resources and Technology Development.

Other companies are experimenting with decentralised management, including the formation of 'quasi-firms' within firms.[6] For example, the Taiwanese electronics firm Acer has divided itself into a network of different businesses, each with its own management, personnel and salary structure. The headquarters employs only 80 people and obtains its revenue from dividends from the separate businesses and from

---

[6] The Matsushita Corporation of Japan combines internal market mechanisms and fierce rivalry between different projects and research groups (Bartlett and Ghoshal, 1990, pp.225-29).

charging other parts of the business for its services. Individual divisions do not have to buy from others within the group and, when they do, they are expected to pay normal market prices (*Economist*, 9 March 1996, p.27). Similarly, ABB[7] has been split into 1,300 quasi-independent units to provide an environment conducive to entrepreneurship within the firm (*Economist*, 10 June 1995, p.79). In the USA the telecommunications giant AT&T recently announced its dissolution into three separate companies (equipment, global information and tele-communications), and Johnson and Johnson, the world's biggest manufacturer of health care products, now consists of 160 disparate businesses operating in 50 countries around the world. Each operating company has considerable management autonomy, far more than would be found in the Taylorist corporation.

Another interesting example is Siemens, the German electrical engineering group, where the company's operating divisions are not obliged to use the services of the company's research laboratories. They are free to subcontract their research and development work to outside organisations (*Financial Times*, 22 October 1996, p.14). This example of the creation of a market within the firm is highly relevant to the main theme of this *Hobart Paper*. It illustrates the lengths to which some companies are going to retain competitiveness. Other examples of expanding firms which use decentralised methods of management include the Massachusetts-based technology group, Thermo-Electron, the German media conglomerate, Bertelsmann, and the California-based comp-uter firm, Hewlett Packard (*Financial Times*, 10 June 1996, p.10).[8]

What many companies now seek is the paradoxical state of 'flexible control'. To compete manufacturers must achieve production methods almost as flexible as those of the pre-industrial, craft era. Under Taylorist production methods the emphasis is on achieving forms of organisation which permit control. But this form of business organisation is challenged by the sheer pace of change in world markets. *All levels* of the

---

[7] ABB (Asea Brown Boveri) is in the electrotechnical business and has over 200,000 employees worldwide.

[8] Also see Halal, Geranmayeh and Pourdehnad (1993).

organisation now need to provide information about the market and *all levels* must contribute to planning and improved production. In an environment where 'clusters' and 'networks' proliferate, there is the potential for considerable information overload and resulting organisational breakdown. Managements therefore are wrestling with how to hold the firm together to ensure a coherent set of business strategies and corporate direction without stultifying the necessary individual creativity and organisational flexibility (Atkinson and Meager, 1986).

Current organisational restructuring to achieve greater flexibility and quality is, in effect, a return to craft-based decentralisation (Hirst and Zeitlin, 1989). Manufacturing flexibility, labour skilling, quality of output and variety of output have all gone through a complete cycle since the start of the Industrial Revolution. Mass production introduced economies of scale but reduced the rôle of craft skills. Taylorism enabled large-scale production but reduced production flexibility and further devalued the individual worker. Atomistic production was replaced by giant, vertically-integrated corporations. Now the inherent bureaucracy and centralised control associated with the huge corporation are seen as obstacles to change (Tirole, 1986). New computer-aided design and manufacture reflect a search for variety and flexibility in manufacture and 'right-first-time' quality.

One related development is the move towards 'flatter' structures through delayering and team-based operations, sometimes of a short-term 'task force' nature (Drucker, 1992). Another is the spread of sub-contracting or outsourcing.[9] Strategic core competencies remain in-house while more is contracted-out to the periphery of the organisation – 'hollowing-out' the corporation to create an organisational form that Charles Handy has likened to a doughnut with in-house, core skills at the centre (Handy, 1994). Outsourcing now accounts for more than one-third of Japanese companies'

---

[9] In terms of the discussion of markets and hierarchies in Section III, Taylorist factories were associated with considerable internal contracting (internal-isation); current trends are leading to much more external contracting (externalisation).

total manufacturing costs (*Economist*, 2 November 1995, p.99).[10]

Under craft production labour skills and intelligence were at a premium. The same is true today in factories and offices. The emphasis now is upon encouraging knowledge acquisition, skills and adaptability in the workforce as critical factors in competitive advantage. Employee commitment, 'multi-tasking' and organisation in self-motivating teams are replacing Taylorist alienation, specialisation and top-down management. At Chrysler's Windsor Plant in Ontario, for example, around 20 per cent of new assembly-line workers are college graduates. Workers are having to make more decisions themselves, middle management having been removed. Chrysler has benefited from reorganising its designers and engineers into 'platform teams' so that manufacturing and marketing of a new model come from the same office. In the computer firm Hewlett Packard in the late 1980s and early 1990s, management remedied problems by cutting the workforce, reducing bureaucracy and encouraging an atmosphere of open communication (*Financial Times*, 10 June 1996, p. 10). Hewlett Packard is also using cross-organisation teams to speed up product development. New product development cycles have been reduced from between two to five years in the late 1980s to as little as six to nine months now.

As firms become looser-coupled, however, and as existing management structures and ways of working are overthrown, an important question arises. How can the firm be held together? Alternatively, how can the need for overall control to prevent anarchy be combined with the degree of flexibility necessary to adapt to changes in the external environment? Flexibility and devolved decision-making seem correct in principle, but ensuring that local units pursue coherent and profitable business strategies then appears difficult. Managers are searching now for forms of communication and control which remove centralised command and control mechanisms

---

[10] According to The Outsourcing Institute of the US, outsourcing spending in the US will have reached US$100 billion in 1996. A survey of several hundred major UK companies has revealed recently that they already outsource a quarter of their budget for what they define as key business processes. Other alternatives to hierarchical organisation include franchising and joint ventures.

that endanger organisational flexibility, yet maintain the coherence and strategic direction of the firm.

The next section examines the nature of the firm in economic analysis before moving on to consider how an understanding of market principles can contribute to solving the apparent conflict between organisational flexibility and control.

III. TRANSACTION COSTS AND CONTRACTING

The early part of this century saw two critical events in the evolution of firms. First was the recognition of the separation of ownership and control in the modern corporation (Berle and Means, 1933) and the second was Taylorism with its command and control model of management (reviewed in the previous section). The separation of ownership and control highlighted the rôle of the professional manager, while Taylorism emphasised the bureaucratic and functional form of organisation as the means to manage the large corporation. In subsequent years management writers and consultants have viewed the firm essentially in terms of the command-and-control paradigm. Resource allocation in the firm has been viewed as qualitatively different from resource allocation in the market-place. Within the firm resources were assumed to be best allocated by management fiat – though rarely was any alternative method of resource allocation considered.

Coase's Starting Point

The appearance of an identifiable dividing line between economic transactions in firms and economic transactions in markets provided the starting point for the analysis of 'The Nature of the Firm' in Ronald Coase's seminal paper of that title (Coase, 1937). Coase developed his interest in why some resources were allocated in markets while other resources were allocated in firms through observation of production processes in the USA, during a year's absence from his studies at the London School of Economics. Later he would write:

> 'What stimulated my interest was that we seemed to lack any theory that would explain why...industries are organised in the way they were. My year in the United States was essentially devoted to a search for a theory of integration.' (Coase, 1991a, p.38.)

Coase's 1937 paper was largely ignored by economists at the time and for many years afterwards. It addressed the question of the existence of the firm at a time when most economists were happy to accept it simply as an assumption within an equilibrium model of the competitive market.[1] Only from the 1960s did the paper (and a complementary paper in 1960 which applied a similar approach to externalities in market economies[2]) achieve the recognition it deserved. In 1991 Coase was awarded the Nobel Prize for economics.

Coase's approach to resource allocation in markets and firms has shaped the subsequent transactions costs and contracts literature, as developed and refined by a number of economists working outside the traditional neo-classical paradigm. Amongst the most notable contributors to this literature have been Alchian and Demsetz (1972), Marschak and Radner (1972), Jensen and Meckling (1976), and especially Oliver Williamson (for example, 1975, 1985). This so-called 'New Institutionalist' literature focuses on the interface between firms and the market and the resulting implications for contracting and performance monitoring. The original 'markets and hierarchies' literature drew a clear boundary between resource allocation in markets and firms resulting from differences in transactions costs. More recently, the notion that there is a sharp distinction between firms and markets has begun to break down (Richardson, 1972; Klein, 1983). There is now far more interest in hybrid forms of organisation involving hierarchies and market signals.

The question with which Coase wrestled was: given that the market economy is generally an excellent means of allocating resources, why do firms exist? When discussed by economists (not very frequently), the question had usually been answered in terms of technological inseparabilities, which meant that certain types of production had to occur in large production

---

[1] The 'theory of the firm' in traditional neo-classical economics is a theory of price and output determination under different competitive conditions. Some economists have defended the theory against those who have criticised it for having a naïve view of the firm (for example, Friedman, 1953; Machlup, 1967). It is true that the theory provides predictions of price movements; it is, however, associated with a serious neglect of the nature of the firm, the subject which Ronald Coase addressed. As Edith Penrose has observed: 'Few economists thought it necessary to enquire what happened inside the firm and indeed their "firm" had no "insides" so to speak.' (Penrose, 1995, p.x: Foreword to the third edition.)

[2] Coase (1960).

units. Coase realised, however, that technological factors and associated economies of scale might explain the existence of large industrial plants but could not explain so easily why the contractual relationship within these plants was one of employment rather than continuous market contracting.

An alternative view is that capitalist firms are a means of exploitation because of the control that capitalists achieve over the production process – an idea central to the older Marxist literature and repeated in its more modern forms and allied writings. In this literature the firm is separate from the market 'acting as a protective enclave from market forces' (Hodgson, 1993, p.91). The capitalist increases his economic power and protects that power by concentrating economic resources within firms (for example, Marglin, 1974; Willman, 1983; Putterman, 1984; Pitelis, 1993, p.268). But an analysis of the distinctions between capitalist firms and capitalist markets cannot progress very far when both are prejudged as complementary parts of an exploitative system. More pertinent is the recent suggestion by Keith Cowling and Roger Sugden (1994) that firms and markets should be viewed from the perspective of strategic decision-making.[3] This approach appears to correspond well with the current trend towards fuzzier and more fluid organisational boundaries.

Contracting for Resources (Transaction Costs)

In Coase's analysis the existence of firms in a market economy is explained in terms of differences in contracting for resources in markets and firms or what have since been labelled *transaction costs*.[4] This offers a much richer approach to analysing the boundary of the firm than either the technological or neo-marxist literatures. Coase argued that the boundary between resource allocation within markets and within 'firms' (a term he used to embrace all organisations) was determined by the relative costs of market and firm

---

[3] Cowling and Sugden use this insight as the basis for an attack on transnational firms and specifically the power relations within such firms and their markets. We differ in seeing it simply as a useful departure point for a discussion of organisations and the rôle of the market.

[4] Coase did not use the term 'transaction costs' in his 1937 paper. Kenneth Arrow appears to have been the first to use the term, in 1969, to describe the 'costs of running the economic system' (Arrow, 1969, p.84).

resource allocation. Where resources could most cost-effectively be allocated in markets, then resources would be so allocated. If it were cheaper to allocate resources within firms then resources would be allocated there. By contrasting markets and firms, Coase suggested there was a sharp distinction in their method of resource allocation which turned on the use of price: 'Outside the firm,...production...is coordinated through a series of transactions on the market. Within a firm those market transactions are eliminated' (Coase, 1937, p.388) and 'It can, I think, be assumed that the distinguishing mark of the firm is the supersession of the price mechanism.' (*ibid.*, p.390.)

Although subsequent 'Coasian' analysis has revolved around the relative costs of transacting in markets and firms, these transaction costs are rarely clearly explained. They were not specified precisely in Coase's paper. There is, however, agreement that they arise from the costs of seeking out buyers and sellers and arranging, policing and enforcing agreements or contracts in a world of imperfect information. For example, in terms of labour input, transaction costs might be reduced by the existence of a firm if an employment contract is written rather than a series of spot market contracts or 'state contingent' contracts.[5] It can be costly to negotiate a series of spot contracts while, by their nature, state contingent contracts can be both costly to write and monitor. Equally, employment contracts enjoy a degree of in-built flexibility as the duties of the employee are usually stated in general terms only. Normally, market contracts work best if the quantity and quality of goods or services and the circumstances of their delivery can be clearly defined. In other words, they work best where the contracts can be complete.

Full contingent claims contracts become more costly to write, monitor and enforce as the degree of uncertainty and complexity in the economic transaction increases. Incomplete long-term contracts are one answer, but these lead to inevitable problems arising out of their incompleteness, which may put at risk the interests of one party or the other. Therefore, in circumstances where it is complex and hence costly to arrange spot contracts or state contingent contracts,

---

[5] State contingent contracts involve actions that should occur if certain events in the future arise.

and there are appreciable transactions costs as a result, resources may be most efficiently allocated within firms. According to the *command view*, firm and market transactions have a fundamental difference that arises from differences in transaction costs. The command structure is one in which resources are allocated without obvious reference to market prices to reduce transaction costs. Hierarchies economise on transaction costs by using partial or incomplete contracts and managerial direction of labour and non-labour inputs and outputs.

Williamson's Contribution

The subsequent literature on firms and markets that has blossomed since the 1960s has largely followed Coase's approach and determined the boundary of the firm and the market through differences in the costs of transacting. A useful comparative contractual approach to studying firms and markets has developed where the transaction is the basic unit of analysis. Much of the research has been concerned with exploring when incomplete contracts will create problems for markets. Some of the most outstanding contributions are by Oliver Williamson who, more than anyone else, has popularised the notion of transaction costs and their contribution to understanding the forms of economic organisation.[6]

In a series of studies, Williamson (for instance, 1975, 1985) concentrated on the distinction between markets and firms (or what he preferred to label 'hierarchies'). Firms are heavily influenced by a desire to maximise economic efficiency and transaction costs are important in determining the most efficient form of organisation, namely market or hierarchy. Transaction costs arise from what Williamson called *bounded rationality, opportunism* and *asset specificity*.[7] The objective then is to organise transactions so as to economise on bounded rationality, while simultaneously safeguarding against the

---

[6] The contribution of Alfred Chandler should also be acknowledged (Chandler, 1962, 1977 and 1990).

[7] Other economists have suggested related arguments. Barzel (1982), for example, talks about organisations existing to reduce measurement costs in economic activity.

hazards that one party or another to the contract might take advantage of its power and act opportunistically.[8]

Through these concepts of bounded rationality, opportunism and asset specificity, Williamson explains the existence of firms in terms of a bilateral dependency (or monopoly) in certain transactions. Bounded rationality relates to the limits to obtaining and processing information.[9] According to Williamson, people are rational in their behaviour, in that they pursue their own well-being (utility) or profit, but they do so in an environment of imperfect information. In other words, people maximise but within the constraint of bounded information, including an imperfect capacity to assimilate and process all available information (an idea equivalent to what is sometimes colloquially called 'information overload').

Williamson uses the term 'opportunism' to refer to 'the incomplete or distorted disclosure of information, especially to calculated efforts to mislead, distort, disguise, obfuscate or otherwise confuse' (Williamson, 1985, pp.47-48). What he alternatively describes as 'self interest seeking with guile' is a product of both bounded rationality and small numbers contracting. More specifically, it refers to the opportunity of one party to a transaction to obtain an advantage 'opportunistically'.

According to Williamson, opportunism in a transaction becomes a particular threat where there is asset specificity. Asset specificity refers to the existence of dedicated assets, both tangible (such as plant and machinery) and intangible (such as know-how and skills).[10] If production is associated

---

[8] Williamson (1985, p.61) argues that the aim is to economise on transaction costs and production costs (for example, through economies of scale and technological inseparabilities). However, transaction costs may affect production costs (and vice versa), therefore separating the two can be a problem.

[9] The work of H.A. Simon (1957, 1972) was important in flagging the rôle of information processing. Information complexity can lead to uncertainty, as in a game of chess where computational ability is a key issue. Limits in terms of both knowledge and powers of calculation lead to bounded rationality (Simon, 1972, p.170) and sometimes to highly complex and unpredictable behaviour (Parker and Stacey, 1994).

[10] Williamson discusses the following types of asset specificity: site specificity, physical specificity and human asset specificity.

with heavy investment in such assets and the costs cannot be recovered except through fulfilment of the contract, then after the investment has occurred scope exists for the other party to the contract to exploit the position (also see Klein, Crawford and Alchian, 1978). In particular, the party to a transaction that invests in an asset and incurs sunk costs may be at a disadvantage in any subsequent renegotiation of the contract; for example, where a television company has invested large amounts in television studios and needs to renew its operating licence.

Similarly, a firm with specific assets may hold an advantage when the other party comes to rely upon it for particular services. For instance, a member of staff with specific skills may be reliant on the firm for employment since those skills are not readily transferable to another firm. Such opportunistic behaviour could also occur where there are information asymmetries, in the sense that one party to the contract is better informed than the other. The supplier of a component, for example, is likely to know much more about its quality and cost than the purchasing firm and could therefore trade opportunistically. The result of opportunistic behaviour may be adverse selection (the *ex ante* choice of an inferior option) or moral hazard (increasing the *ex post* risk that one party will exploit the terms of the contract to the disadvantage of the other party).[11]

According to Williamson, organising resources within hierarchies can reduce the opportunism that might be associated with market exchange. By cultivating a common purpose and through authority controls (for example, the rule book and the threat of dismissal) opportunistic behaviour might be kept in check. Equally, adaptive, sequential decision-making in hierarchies may reduce problems arising from bounded rationality, while at the same time avoiding repeated spot-market contracting that could be very costly.[12]

---

[11] Williamson includes both adverse selection and moral hazard in what he terms 'information impactedness' leading to opportunistic behaviour. Of course, given uncertainty, what seems to be opportunistic behaviour may simply occur because of different perceptions of the world on the part of those entering into the contracting (Langlois, 1984).

[12] Williamson goes on to emphasise both the incompleteness of the employment contract and the rôle of the internal capital market as keys to an understanding of the benefits from resource allocation in hierarchies. In addition to task

Organising resource allocation within firms also has costs, however – the costs of management or internal control of resources. These costs can be expected to rise as the firm grows in size and puts strains on centralised management.[13] In the markets and hierarchies literature there is a clear trade-off between market transaction costs and internal management costs. If these management costs are treated as the transaction costs of resource allocation *within* firms, the decision as to whether to allocate resources within firm or markets reduces to one of the *relative* transaction costs. Ignoring other (production) costs associated with firms, resources will be most efficiently allocated internally when the market transaction costs exceed the transaction costs of internalisation. [14]

---

flexibility, employment can be a means of locking-in employees who have strategic information and/or high (sunk) training costs. Williamson argues that the internal capital market may result in cost savings in terms of the raising and allocating of capital, a view that is especially controversial where external capital markets are well developed.

[13] Williamson sees the multi-divisional firm as a development that occurred to overcome rising management costs as firms expanded (see Williamson, 1991, p.105.) Williamson also analyses the case for vertical integration in terms of transaction cost economising.

[14] This is Williamson's argument. However, we do not suggest that transaction cost economics is a *sufficient* theory of economic organisation. It is not essential to our argument about applying market principles within firms. We accept that transaction cost economics alone may not be able to explain the dynamics of institutional change because of its concern with costs and relative neglect of possible benefits from different forms of resource allocation (for example, the benefits in terms of supernormal profits or monopolisation of markets): '...if benefits are acknowledged it introduces the possibility that inefficient governance structures may exist (in the sense of costs being higher than feasible alternatives), and efficient structures may not exist.' (Dietrich, 1994, p.37.) We also accept that the firm should be viewed as a 'production' as well as an 'exchange' environment. There must, of course, be production for firms to exist (exchange could not occur without production for in its absence what would there be to exchange?) and it is important to appreciate that management actions can change production costs and revenues and not just transaction costs. Internalisation of transactions may raise control costs but achieve a more than offsetting benefit through higher profit potential (again, for instance, in the case of monopolisation of markets through certain production arrangements). Using notation from Dietrich (*ibid.*, pp.79-80) where Bm is benefits from market contracting, Bf is benefits from intra-firm resource allocation, Cm is market transaction costs, and Cf is internal (organisational) costs, the choice of in-house activity requires that: $(Bf-Cf) > (Bm-Cm)$.

More recently, Williamson has recognised the need to address intermediate forms of organisation between markets and hierarchies. Intermediate forms encompass organisations with blurred boundaries resulting from the contracting out of non-core functions, entering into joint ventures and establishing semi-autonomous operating units – Charles Handy's doughnut organisation. These developments, discussed in Section II, blur any clear distinction between resource allocation in the market and by command (or hierarchy). A clear distinction between firms and markets, as suggested in much of the early markets and hierarchies literature, might have been appropriate to a Taylorist world, but is much less relevant today.

Furthermore, it is far from obvious that the border between the firm and the market was ever as distinct as the earlier literature implied. There has always been considerable similarity between contracting for services and direct employment of inputs (Ouchi, 1980). In both cases contracts are entered into, though the details of the contract and the likely frequency of recontracting differ. Moreover, in both cases, within the terms of the contract either party can usually terminate it. Arguably, therefore, the differences between markets and hierarchies are best analysed in terms of *a unified theory of contracts and incentives* rather than as fundamentally different institutional structures. As Steven Cheung (1983) has argued, when transactions are internalised: 'it is *not* quite correct to say the "firm" supersedes "the market". Rather, one type of contract supersedes another type.' The contract between the restaurant owner who hires a carpenter to make a new worktop and the contract between the restaurant owner and the cook employed in the kitchen differ in terms of their length, the terms they dictate, and the payment schemes they embody. They are different contracts; but they are both contracts.

Transaction/Hierarchy or Bureaucratic Costs

Transaction costs emphasise the possible benefits of hierarchy, whereas agency theory focuses on minimising its bureaucratic costs. In Jensen and Meckling's landmark paper on agency problems, they projected the essence of the firm as one of contractual relationships:

'The private corporation or firm is simply one form of legal fiction which serves as a nexus for contracting relationships... Viewed this way, it makes little or no sense to try to distinguish those things which are "inside" the firm... from those things that are "outside" of it. There is in a very real sense only a multitude of complex relationships (i.e. contracts) between the legal fiction (the firm) and the owners of labour, materials and capital inputs and the consumers of output.' (Jensen and Meckling, 1976, pp.310-11.)

In a subsequent paper, Sanford Grossman and Oliver Hart (1986) extended this analysis in terms of incomplete contracting. In their study the ownership of assets was associated with residual rights of control over their use, that is to say, rights freely to use assets other than as set down in the contract. Grossman and Hart focused on physical assets rather than control of employees within firms, though their analysis can be extended to the latter. The costs of integrating within firms are analysed in terms of residual rights and not bureaucracy costs.

In this view, the organisation is essentially a 'nexus of contracts' between the employer, employees, suppliers of capital, providers of raw materials and component suppliers and buyers. The firm is a legal fiction if it is seen to be distinct from this nexus which forms the governance structure, in which all the agents that make up transactions in firms (employees, management, capital providers and perhaps other suppliers) exist. So influential has this contracts view of the firm become, that in one of Oliver Williamson's more recent papers he has stressed that firms and markets are 'alternative modes for organising the very same transaction' (Williamson, 1991, p.4). The different governance structures or contract forms are selected according to their relative efficiencies in terms of transaction costs.

Viewing the firm in terms of contracts means focusing less on the differences between transactions, as in Coase's analysis and the early markets and hierarchies view of the firm, and more on the similarities between the contracts that make up the firm. A 'contract view' of the firm, in contrast to the 'command' view, emphasises similarities rather than differences between resource allocation in firms and in markets.[15] By so doing it provides a basis for the application of market principles to resource allocation within the firm. Once it is recognised that firms and markets are similar rather than different, it becomes obvious that resource allocation methods that have proved their worth in the external market might have application within the firm, if after some adaptation.

From a contracts view, the economics of firms does not differ sharply from the economics of markets. There is no 'firm mode of organisation' or 'firm mode of resource allocation' separate and distinct from the market mode. Both firms and markets entail contracts, the firm differing only in the nature of those contracts. Whereas Coase distinguished sharply between intra-firm and inter-firm transactions, the former depending upon hierarchy, the contracts view of the firm allows for the possibility that intra-firm transactions can have market-like relationships (Klein, 1983, p.373).

The Management Problem

Transactions cost economics and the complementary literature on the economics of contracting provide a rich analysis of the nature of firms and the allocation of resources in markets and hierarchies. An appreciation of the costs of transacting in markets compared with resource allocation in firms provides the basis for reconsidering the rôle of market principles within firms. The literature may not as yet provide a comprehensive explanation for the existence of the firm (Pitelis, 1993; Dietrich, 1994). But, whatever its shortcomings in terms of explaining why firms exist, the Coasian view, as amended and expanded by the markets and hierarchies and contracts literatures, has opened up the 'black box' of the firm. Far more economists are now concerned with what goes on within firms than a generation ago. The contracts view has led economists to focus on the nature of relationships within and around firms, including governance structures. Of particular concern are incentive mechanisms in the supply chain and relationships between both suppliers of capital and appointed managers, and management and the labour force.

---

[15] The view of the firm as a nexus of contracts, essentially no different in this respect from market transactions, is defended in Cheung (1983). See also Richardson (1972) and Fama (1980).

Unlike Coase's original paper which was concerned with the distinction between firms and markets, in recent years the similarities between resource allocation in markets and firms have been stressed. Both forms of contracting involve problems of incentives and motivation. Coase now acknowledges that he neglected the issue of how to organise resources within firms to reduce transaction costs:[16]

'I emphasised [in the 1937 article] the comparison of the costs of transacting with the costs of organising and did not investigate the factors that would make the costs of organising lower for some firms than for others. This was quite satisfactory if the main purpose was, as mine was, to explain why there are firms. But if one is to explain the institutional structure of production in the system as a whole it is necessary to uncover the reasons why the cost of organising particular activities differs among firms.' (Coase, 1991a, p.73.)

The case for hierarchical forms of organisation can be made in terms of economising on transaction costs (Casson, 1994). There is an inherent division of labour in information gathering and processing because members of the firm have different exposures to market conditions, production and marketing processes and input suppliers. Hence the importance of effective communication to minimise communication and investigation costs and to maximise the potential benefits. Viewed in this way, the rôle of senior management is both to encourage efficient collection and use of information within the organisation and to recognise profit opportunities in the market when contracting for outputs and inputs.[17]

Considering the firm as a resource allocator using contracts and including the rôle of residual rights focuses attention on the costs of managing resources.[18] For instance, to return to

---

[16] Coase has conceded that in his original paper he placed too much emphasis upon the employment relationship as the distinguishing feature of firms (Coase, 1991a). He also recognises now that there are firms with internal markets co-ordinating transactions using prices, so that the distinction between firms and markets is blurred (Coase, 1991b, p.55).

[17] For a similar view of the entrepreneur, see Casson (1982).

[18] Inherent to the following discussion is the agent-principal relationship, in which the principals are residual risk-takers (Fama and Jensen, 1983).

the restaurant example, hiring the carpenter on a full-time basis creates a potential shirking problem, as Alchian and Demsetz (1972), for example, recognised. If, in particular, the quantity and quality of output are difficult to monitor, the employee may be especially inclined to shirk, to the point that the economies from employment are more than offset by shirking costs. This undesirable outcome must be addressed through changes in incentives and information.[19] It cannot, of course, be solved simply through changes in how the contractual relationship is labelled (for example, consultant or employee, market or firm, master or servant). The problems of managing a firm then appear analogous to the problems of central planning.

In other words, the decision as to whether to produce in-house or contract out revolves around the *total* of production and transaction costs, including the costs of shirking and management (agency) costs. The transaction costs literature has highlighted the importance of the institutional setting in which exchanges occur and hence in the evolution and rationale of comparative institutions. Although there are similarities between firms and markets from a contracts perspective, the substitution of market for in-house contracts involves a change in the *nature* of the business and more specifically in the degree of control and residual rights.

The rôle of senior management is to set out the strategic direction of the firm and establish an internal organisation conducive to adapting according to changing external signals. Management may be motivated by rights to the residual (profit) or by the payment of bonuses and salaries agreed with those who hold the property rights (that is, shareholders). However, it is the workforce that ultimately achieves corporate success by producing the right quality and amount of the goods or services demanded in the market. To steer the business, senior management needs to provide some form of regulation or self-regulation to achieve effective working, including an incentive system to ensure appropriate and timely adjustment to the external environment. At the same time, it has to be recognised that senior management is capable of inhibiting change through inappropriate inter-

---

[19] This management problem also helps to explain the existence of hierarchies in status and control within organisations.

ventions. This reasoning extends beyond the employment of labour to the purchase of all factor inputs, including new investment. In particular, *ex post* rights to the capital must be tailored to provide necessary *ex ante* incentives for senior management to perform its task efficiently.[20]

People respond to the carrot as well as the stick and hence most firms appreciate the value of cultivating loyalty and high performance from their employees by using appropriate incentives. Obviously senior management gives instructions to the workforce rather than the other way round. But instead of seeing this asymmetry in terms of economic power (as in Marxist and allied literature), the contracts view focuses on shirking and incentive reasons for the chain of command (see especially Alchian and Demsetz, 1972).[21]

The next section looks first at specific examples of the rôle that market principles can play in the running of firms, and then at the nature of incentives within firms. The principles developed are appropriate to changes now underway in companies which are leading to flatter organisational structures, more operating autonomy at the local level and the empowerment of employees.

---

[20] Here we use the term 'senior management': alternatively in some firms the term 'entrepreneur' may be more appropriate. Below we use the two terms interchangeably even though we recognise that some economists prefer to separate out the input of enterprise from the input of management. In our view senior management in modern corporations must be entrepreneurial if their firms are to prosper.

[21] In Section IV we discuss the rôle of incentives, including culture, routines, procedures and the like, in producing behaviour conducive to the achievement of corporate objectives. Also, see Casson (1994).

IV. MARKET PRINCIPLES AND THE FIRM: SOME APPLICATIONS

Micro-economics does not provide a recipe for the correct organisation of production. Rather, economic tools provide us with concepts for understanding organisational and managerial issues. The primary managerial dilemmas involve the discovery, mobilisation, and integration of dispersed knowledge. As Hayek once observed:

> 'The economic problem of society is...a problem of how to secure the best use of resources known to any of the members of society, for ends whose relative importance only these individuals know...It is a problem of utilitisation of knowledge.' (Hayek, 1945, pp.519-20.)[1]

We take the same perspective on the economic problem of the firm. In this section we show how an emphasis on knowledge problems can provide fruitful insights into management. We start with an examination of Koch Industries, one firm that has been particularly successful in applying market economics to its managerial practice. We then consider some more general applications of market economics to management, including the rôle of prices within the firm, the function of management and the rôle of incentives.

Koch Industries Inc.

Management at Koch Industries Inc., based in Wichita, Kansas, has been applying Hayekian ideas to the real world evidently with considerable success, using market economics to unlock the problems of management (see *Wall Street Journal*, 18 April 1997). Charles Koch, chairman and CEO since 1967, has even coined and trademarked the term 'Market-Based Management'® – to express the company's management philosophy and practice.

---

[1] Much later Hayek observed: '... the most important rôle of the market is that of a device for the transmission and utilisation of unarticulated, and sometimes inarticulable, tacit and local knowledge' (Hayek, 1978, p.8). Our argument is that potentially this is as true within organisations as outside.

Koch Industries Inc. is a US petroleum company which gathers, transports, processes, and trades oil (it performs only a limited amount of exploration and production, and owns no service stations). The company has also expanded into a variety of related areas, including oil refining, petrochemicals, natural gas and gas liquids, asphalt, sulphur products, ammonia, cattle feed, farm service centres, and chemical technology products. The company's success has been astonishing. During the past 25 years its revenues have grown more than 100-fold to over US$20 billion. Koch Industries is now one of the largest privately-owned firms in America.

Charles Koch and other senior managers attribute the success of the business to its application of the principles of market economics. Koch has said:

> 'Market-Based Management means internalising the beneficial characteristics of a free market economy, and eliminating the harmful effects of a command economy. It's difficult in practice, because we can't just copy everything from the external market – we have to adapt market principles for use inside the firm.' (Cited in Cowen and Ellig, 1995, p.1.)

The Koch Industries vision of 'Market-Based Management'® can be broken down into three parts: mission, organisational structure, and incentive mechanisms. Each is examined below.

Corporate mission statements are statements of purpose and overall direction. The mission of Koch Industries is process-based, unlike many other corporate missions. The mission is continuously analysed, discussed, and refined to respond to changing circumstances. In many other businesses, in contrast, the mission is posted up (and then largely ignored) for years on end. It is rarely remembered and respected by lower levels of management and the shop-floor workforce. Koch Industries' process of continuous mission refinement is used to generate ongoing information about the firm's comparative advantages and how well it has succeeded in translating those advantages into profit.

Koch Industries also requires each business unit, and indeed each individual, to develop its own mission to support the corporation's overall mission, thereby spreading 'ownership' of corporate objectives. These missions are used to guide day-to-day decisions. They serve as a set of principles which economise on information and help alleviate co-ordination problems within the firm. Individual missions help business divisions and individuals discover their own comparative advantages, and give benchmarks that can be used to judge their performances, whilst maintaining the strategic direction of the organisation.

The second aspect of Market-Based Management® at Koch Industries concerns organisational structure. Ongoing re-organisations have split the company into discrete business units ('profit centres') with their own profit and loss statements. Profit centres are created when senior management spots a group of individuals and activities where the benefits of teamwork and co-operation appear especially large. Profit-centre leaders are then responsible for running their operations like a separate business, albeit with overall corporate monitoring to prevent damage to the long-run interests of the corporation as a whole. Organisation into profit centres liberates managers from the inefficiencies of detailed central direction, and allows the firm to reap the benefits of decentralised information. It is increasingly used by other corporations (see Section II).

Both inside and across profit centres, Koch Industries uses cross-functional teams, the members of which may be drawn from different parts of the firm and may come together only temporarily or for specific projects. The widespread use of these teams replaces the fixed organisational structure of the more traditional business firm. The organisational form in Koch Industries is built explicitly upon the recognition that the mobilisation and integration of scattered knowledge should drive the allocation of tasks and responsibilities.

Another Koch Industries practice redraws traditional hierarchical notions of responsibility using a form of matrix management. Rather than connecting each individual to another individual higher in the corporate hierarchy, matrix management draws multiple and crossing links of authority and responsibility. Each individual is accountable to several persons rather than to a single manager. Similarly, each business unit can have responsibilities to several other business units. Matrix management recognises that information flows are not always predictable or uni-directional in the modern corporation. Employees also develop a greater sense of their ultimate accountability to the consumer of the firm's products and to the firm's mission, rather than to some specific individual known as a 'boss'.

The third aspect of Market-Based Management® involves the proper specification of incentives. Senior Koch Industries management often speak of 'defining property rights within the firm'. Missions and organisational structures will not bring business success unless they are supported by a proper set of incentives. Market-Based Management® portrays mission, organisational structure, and incentives as a unified package. The mission process provides information about what should be achieved, organisational structure gives individuals the necessary co-operative means to achieve that end, and incentives provide the motivation.

The use of incentives to improve business performance is common in corporate life, but viewing the problem of performance in terms of Market-Based Management® has allowed Koch Industries to enjoy an unusual degree of success in this regard. Koch Industries' incentive compensation system, which covers middle and upper-level management, emphasises the discovery of knowledge. Although the total size of the bonus pool for a business group depends upon its financial performance, senior management tries to avoid situations where individuals distort information or engage in 'turf wars' to maximise the size of their bonuses. Bonuses are awarded on the basis of the discovery and sharing of knowledge, contribution towards the long-run profitability of the corporation, and an individual's efforts to develop and implement the mission at Koch Industries.

Mission statements, matrix forms of management and incentives are fairly commonplace in industry. What marks out Koch Industries is the way they are integrated using a 'mental mapping' of the organisation based on market principles. The application of market principles to management at Koch Industries serves as an integrated approach to analysing and evaluating business proposals. Charles Koch has written:

'Our experience has shown that market-based management is a framework within which we can analyse, and even improve upon, other management concepts such as Total Quality Management and Re-engineering. By testing these ideas and programs against the principles of market-based management, we are better able to discern which parts truly add value and then apply them in a manner that is consistent and complementary with our other

51

ongoing efforts. This helps us to avoid the "false start" and "flavor of the month" problems that have plagued so many other companies and management approaches.' (Foreword by Charles Koch to Gable and Ellig, 1993, pp.2-3.)

Koch Industries' experience demonstrates the practical benefits to be gained from applying market economics to management. In Koch Industries, and in a number of other firms, internal markets are providing powerful incentives to maximise efficiency in resource use (Ellig, 1993). The development of buy-sell relationships amongst 'teams', 'clusters' and business units can produce a true spirit of enterprise. In an internal market every business unit operates as a 'quasi-independent' activity, buying in-house and out-sourcing according to the relative economic advantages. Prices play a much bigger rôle in determining the flow of resources within the organisation than in the Taylorist firm with its command or planning structures.[2]

The company's experience also demonstrates that market principles need to be carefully applied within the firm and not imported without relevant changes or refinement. If the firm is viewed simply as a market or a series of markets then the rationale for the firm's existence disappears. The transaction cost advantages of the firm over the market are lost if the firm simply becomes a market. In particular, within the organisation 'public' (company wide) and 'private' (local business unit) objectives and rates of return may diverge because private decision-makers are unable to appropriate all of the benefits they create or do not internalise all of the costs they generate. In other words, actions in one part of a business may 'spillover' into the activities of another part and the consequence can be a failure to internalise all costs and benefits in the internal prices used.

---

[2] See 'Barclays finds healthy interest in its IT expertise', *Management Today*, March 1996, p. 74. When three years ago Barclays Bank in the UK allowed each of its 30 businesses to decide on commercial grounds where to go for computer services, the in-house computer department began to compete for work with outside contractors. Economists, aware of the importance of prices and competition, will not be surprised to learn that the performance of the bank's computer department improved to such an extent that it now not only services bank users, it also competes successfully for the IT work of a number of other blue-chip companies.

In setting internal prices, the full opportunity cost of resource use within the firm should be considered and prices set on that basis. Equally, as in the case of Koch Industries, the mission statement, along with supporting procedures and routines, should be seen as a co-ordinating mechanism or a parameter setter.[3] The mission (however articulated), procedures and routines should advance values and priorities which individuals within the firm respect and to which they react positively. They then provide a framework for action not dissimilar to the rôles of the rule of law, conventions and norms of behaviour and trust in the wider economy. As explained below, in the market economy and within the firm 'social order' is essential for efficient economic transacting.

The Rôle of Prices within the Firm

Command and hierarchy views of the business firm typically emphasise a trade-off between economising upon transactions costs and using the price system. This distinction dates from Coase (1937) and Williamson (1975), as explained in Section III. According to this view, the creation of a business firm may decrease transactions costs, but firm owners must forego the price system for their productive activities. 'Low-powered' (bureaucratic) incentives replace the 'high-powered' incentives of markets. Once a business firm is created, the owners supposedly must allocate resources as would a central planner. At the extreme, market prices do not and cannot indicate how resources should be allocated 'within the firm'.

Focusing on the similarities between firms and markets instead of the differences, as we did towards the end of the previous section, provides the basis for an alternative view, that firms need not sacrifice the use of prices. Individuals within organisations can allocate inputs by observing external market prices and by estimating internal (subjective) opportunity costs. Individuals 'outside' firms do not have access to any special kind of information that those 'inside' firms cannot also obtain.

At the same time, management should take account of the likelihood that market prices will not measure the exact internal opportunity cost of a resource. But a possible

---

[3] Routines enable actions and conduct without conscious thought or explicit instruction.

disparity between price and economic opportunity cost holds for all resource allocation decisions, whether in 'firms' or 'markets'. The disparity between market price and internal opportunity cost results from the subjectivity of value, and is not unique to the firm mode of organisation.

Moving away from the firms-markets dichotomy, as we did in Section III, provides a fresh perspective on the use of transfer or 'internal' (shadow) prices. By using a set of (shadow) price signals to decision-makers located in profit or cost centres (for instance, departments and subsidiaries) of the firm, the firm can mimic the market mechanism. Plans and actions of each decision-maker are matched so as to achieve (ideally) some form of optimal co-ordination. Transfer prices are not an imperfect substitute when a real market does not exist but a universally-present attempt to measure internal opportunity cost, and to express that cost in some comparable form. An emphasis on the economics of contracting also offers a new slant on how to evaluate transfer prices. Rather than trying to develop transfer prices which mimic market prices, as standard approaches to transfer pricing suggest, the focus should be on why transfer prices should *differ* from external market prices.

For purposes of contrast, consider the traditional approach to transfer pricing[4] which starts with the perfectly competitive market as a benchmark for fixing transfer prices. Ideally, entrepreneurs are supposed to calculate transfer prices by taking a price from a competitive market where that input is traded. Transfer price analysts do recognise that perfectly competitive prices for inputs generally do not exist; in that case they suggest extrapolating transfer prices from whatever market prices can be found, after adjusting for any differences in the quality of the inputs.

In our view, transfer prices perform a somewhat different function. Competitive market prices measure opportunities for external exchange. Transfer prices, in contrast, should attempt to measure the *subjective* opportunity cost of the firm's resources. Hence, they involve an inherent degree of subjectivity and firm-specific information. These internal opportunity costs can and will differ systematically from

---

[4] For an introduction to and discussion of internal (shadow) pricing, see Buckley and Casson (1976); Vancil (1978); Eccles (1985); and Hennart (1991a).

market prices. Senior management purchase a particular set of resources precisely because those resources have special value to the firm, or can be deployed in some new and innovative way. Transfer prices should reflect the value of the resources to the firm, rather than the value of the resources to the outside market, whether perfectly competitive or not.

To the extent that a firm has a comparative knowledge advantage in using or owning a resource, the transfer or internal price for a resource should stand above market levels. In other words, firms should value their resources at above their measured market values – otherwise, why are those resources acquired? Attempting to base transfer prices on market prices is likely to underestimate 'correct' transfer prices.

The traditional view of transfer prices, based on the perfectly competitive model, sees spot market exchange as allocating resources through the use of market prices, whereas firms supersede the price mechanism. Transfer prices are an imperfect substitute for the market prices that disappear when the firm is created. The contracts approach to the business firm, in contrast, turns attention to the necessary difference between market prices and internal measures of opportunity cost – the very motivation for the firm's existence in the first place.

Market economics does not provide a mechanistic or replicable recipe for estimating internal opportunity costs. Business managers know that estimating opportunity costs and transfer prices is much easier said than done. In practice, transfer prices are often determined by negotiation across company divisions, or are simply imposed by managers. Internalisation of transaction costs means that a balance has to be struck between internal pricing (shadow prices) and management direction as means of allocating the organisation's resources. Our case is that the application of principles from market economics can provide general guidelines for informing these negotiations, and for evaluating their success. Internalisation need not imply hierarchical (command) controls; instead, considerable autonomy can be given to subsidiaries or teams which have the benefit of knowledge of local production techniques and market conditions.[5] Internal pricing can help to reduce organisational costs and maintain corporate coherence despite the implied decentralised decision-making. Of course, measurement and accounting problems and interdependencies within the organisation restrict the application of internal pricing (Hennart, 1991a). Nevertheless, used with care, internal-market signals can help to allocate resources efficiently, just as they do in the external market.

Corporations have used transfer prices with increasing frequency over the last decade or so (Halal, Geranmayeh and Pourdehnad, 1993; Gable and Ellig, 1993, p.41). Nonetheless, firms often allocate resources without any estimate of the internal opportunity costs, especially in the case of corporate services, such as accounting, purchasing, and personnel. Business units often pay a fixed price or 'tax' to the centre for these services and the resulting organisational structure provides no incentive to the user or supplier to allocate and use those resources efficiently. In consequence, the resources are typically over-used and allocated to less important uses. Producers of overhead services, pressed to meet increasing demands, then cry out for more resources to expand further. If these demands are met, senior management is sinking more resources into an inefficient operation in internal opportunity cost terms. The firm's resources could be better used. Measuring internal opportunity costs, despite its inevitable transactions costs, can help alleviate such problems.[6]

---

[5] Buckley (1983, 1988) draws a distinction between the application of transaction cost analysis in multinational companies (internalisation) and that developed by Williamson (markets and hierarchies). He argues that internalisation need not imply hierarchy because considerable autonomy can be given to subsidiary companies. Buckley advocates shadow prices to reduce the organisational costs that arise when decision-making is decentralised in this way.

[6] One objection to internal pricing relates to the competition within the firm that might result. However, there is much confused thinking about competition in some of the management literature. This is evident, for example, in Rosabeth Moss Kanter's management best seller, when she writes that internal competition can be destructive: 'The first sign that competition has become destructive is that the *players pay more attention to beating their rivals than to performing the task well*...Winning – or avoiding losing – becomes more important than doing the job well.' (Kanter, 1990, pp.76-77, emphasis in original.) This argument entirely misses the point. 'Performing the task well' is precisely the way to beat rivals in a competitive market. Firms that succeed in competitive markets 'do the job well'. Another objection to the use of internal

56

The Rôle of Enterprise and Management

Use of internal pricing does not remove a need for a locus of authority in organisations. Instead, market economics, with its emphasis on knowledge and institutions, enables us to reconceptualise the rôle of the entrepreneur and senior management in a business firm. The entrepreneur and senior management first recognise when factors of production have a complementary function, and then try to create an environment conducive to learning and organisational adaptation for those factors. Their rôle is also to maintain an overall corporate coherence. Decentralisation removes an over-involvement by headquarters in decision-making that reduces the benefits of the division of labour for the collection and processing of information. Competition between divisions and teams within the firm can also act as an important incentive mechanism. At the same time, however, the firm must avoid under-investment in divisions resulting from a concentration on localised risks that are diversified away at the corporate level; an over-narrow focus on the short-run interests of the division over the long-run interests of the whole corporation; and the manipulation of accounting figures to gain internal advantage.

Creation of a learning environment places the entrepreneur or senior management in a planning rôle only in a limited sense. The entrepreneur or senior management establish the governance structures, procedures and routines for the organisation; these procedures and routines should clearly define the general way in which the firm goes about its day-to-day operations.[7] The property rights relate to the framework and arrangements (laws) in which transactions take place. But senior management should not attempt to plan the organisation's future in a rigid sense, nor should it attempt to control each and every action of their workforce. Such planning attempts would likely fail for precisely the same

---

pricing relates to the costs of administering the accounting systems. However, modern IT is removing much of the complexity of internal book-keeping. Also, any remaining costs have to be balanced against the usually high administrative costs of the command and control structure and its other inefficiencies.

7   Transaction cost economics is, of course, essentially concerned with issues of governance. For an excellent discussion of the importance of 'routines' in market economies see Nelson and Winter (1982).

reasons that central economic planning has a poor track record around the world.

The model of perfect competition, which has exercised great influence over neo-classical economics, has perfect information, zero transaction costs, fully secure property rights, and thus no need for the entrepreneur (Kirzner, 1997). The perfectly competitive firm is no more than a production function without organisation, co-ordination, monitoring and measuring costs. Production is simply a matter of enacting the appropriate contracts, and the function of management is to select the profit-maximising outputs and inputs. In the face of perfect information or well-defined probabilistic relationships, management becomes a mere routine of calculation.

As Frank Knight (Knight, 1921) and Joseph Schumpeter (Schumpeter, 1934) pointed out many years ago, however, such static constructs cannot reproduce the complexity of a true market economy. The lack of complete information makes management more than simply a matter of routine co-ordination:

> 'With uncertainty present doing things, the actual execution of activity becomes in a real sense a secondary part of life; the primary problem or function is deciding what to do and how to do it.' (Knight, 1921.)

In practice, the institutional framework affects both production and transaction costs.[8] Entrepreneurs must seek out new markets, new products, and new understandings of the marketing environment. These entrepreneurial functions would be redundant if information were not costly to generate, process, interpret, and disseminate. Entrepreneurs and senior management have to undertake all these tasks, or delegate authority by appointing other persons to undertake them.

---

[8] The notion of 'equilibrium', which is central to neo-classical theorising about market economies, implies that all facts relevant to economic transacting are known and the discovery of new ones has ceased. In fact, however, a market economy is in perpetual motion and new facts are continuously being created. Viewing the market economy as a process leads to the more useful concept of markets as discovery opportunities (Kirzner, 1985). Or, as one anonymous referee commented succinctly: 'Competition is about the evolution of new forms of organisation and not merely the achievement of some static optimum allocation of resources.' We could not agree more.

These activities are costly, and will be undertaken only when there are adequate rewards which require well-defined and generally accepted property rights – in particular, rights to the residual, on the lines set out by Alchian and Demsetz (1972) and developed by Jensen and Meckling (1976) and others. Top management as strategic decision-makers set the mission and design and monitor the performance of the organisation.[9] They contract for the right to hire and fire, invest or disinvest, and expand or contract the organisation. They also contract for the property rights to sell the firm to another firm or to close the firm down altogether. Within the large corporation, the entrepreneurial function is undertaken by senior management; its task is to provide a governance structure that assists the discovery of information to facilitate organisational learning and adaptability, and enables people within the organisation to use this information to ensure the most efficient adaptation and response to external market signals. To this end senior management must define and protect localised property rights within the firm so those rights can be exercised.

The proper rôle of management can be understood in terms of the division of labour. The acquisition and use of knowledge is critical to the success of a business firm, yet it would be uneconomic for everyone in the firm to attempt to acquire and use this knowledge. Similarly, a given piece of knowledge will not have the same impact on all sections of the firm, any more than it has the same effects in all parts of a market. The learning process involved in the acquisition and use of knowledge should be, at one level, centralised within management. At the same time, however, that knowledge should be diffused to those areas of the firm where it will provide the greatest benefit.

Therefore the leading-edge corporation can be described as a polyarchy, to use Michael Polanyi's term (Polanyi, 1951). A polyarchy is a decentralised system where the multiple parts co-ordinate their behaviour through voluntary agreements. In

---

[9] We are not necessarily endorsing the economic, social or other processes that led to some people being managers and strategic decision-makers and others not. But there needs to be *someone* who takes responsibility for the entrepreneurial function or strategic decision-making without which the firm (and the economy) would flounder. Marxists are, of course, extremely critical of the historical process that led to the current distribution of property rights.

so far as individuals freely contract with the firm to provide their services, and in doing so agree to conform to managerial directions, employment in the firm is a voluntary activity. Equally, suppliers of capital, contractors with the firm, and other input suppliers all enter into contracts for capital and services as they see fit. The resulting collection of autonomous individuals is held together by the organisation of the firm, its mission, procedures and routines, as well as by contracts.

If we were to contrast the firm to an organism, the organisation should be like an octopus with a multitude of tentacles tapped into the external environment at various levels. On the end of each tentacle should be an appropriate management structure to ensure effective and efficient diffusion. In the relatively small head of the octopus lie the entrepreneurs, senior management or strategic decision-makers. They have the task of interpreting information about final success or failure, co-ordinating the tentacles and giving the entire organisation a sense of direction.

In this sense, once again, the well-managed firm is more similar to the market than different from it. Just as in a market economy there must be certain rules and norms of behaviour (for example, accepted laws of contract and traditions of trust),[10] so this is true of resource organisation within the firm. In particular, it is a primary rôle of management to prevent the organisation collapsing into anarchy, a possibility more likely perhaps now that organisations are becoming flatter and team working, clusters and networks are developing (see Section II).

---

[10] 'There is an element of trust in every transaction...' (Arrow, 1973, p.23.) On the rôle of trust also see Arrow (1974) and Fox (1974). Ouchi (1980), in describing new forms of organisational structure, talks about 'clan' type organisations within hierarchies based on trust and long-term relationships rather than self-seeking and the need for effective monitoring. Similarly, networking involves trust and co-operation. Such 'quasi-integration' can be seen as an attempt to get the benefits of internalisation (reduced transaction costs) while reducing its costs (management costs). Boisot (1995) also draws attention to clans and networks in his discussion of information and institutions. He provides an informational interpretation of cultural evolution and one in which non-market institutional forms are complements rather than alternatives to markets.

Markets of all kinds involve much more than atomistic rivals operating in intense competition with one another. Markets typically involve an institution-rich mix of competition and collaboration, both within firms and across firms.[11] A market economics perspective on management does not imply the exclusive use of competitive bidding or spot markets within firms, as we have seen. Management usually prefers to lay down the structure and terms of co-operation among the inputs they contract for, rather than arranging all activity along the lines of auction or spot markets. Market economics neither favours nor disfavours atomistic decentralisation within the firm. It provides an overall framework for determining the most profitable degree of decentralisation. Resources should go to those individuals or teams or units with the most appropriate means, incentives, and knowledge to carry out the relevant transactions most efficiently. Internal prices and resulting localised profits and losses provide useful (though not necessarily complete or decisive) information about where resources are best directed.

The McDonald's Formula

The American fast food chain McDonald's provides an interesting example of how a successful operation can embody both extreme centralisation and extreme decentralisation. McDonald's is an extraordinarily loose combination of thousands of different managed restaurants and franchised outlets, scattered all over the world. Yet on some matters, such as the kind of French fries used or the degree of cleanliness, McDonald's senior management tries to remove all discretion from the individual operating units. While this form of centralised direction undoubtedly sacrifices some useful local knowledge, presenting a uniform product and level of quality removes a threat to the McDonald's brand name and the informational burden on potential customers – the relevant knowledge problem in this case. Consumers can rely upon receiving a standard service at each and every McDonald's restaurant. This centralised direction is dropped, however, when it is not dictated by requirements of brand protection and knowledge. For instance, McDonald's gives its franchisees

---

[11] For a valuable insight into the complementary rôles of competition and collaboration in market economies, see Burton (1996).

almost unlimited latitude to conduct the local marketing campaigns.[12]

The institutions within the firm hold anarchy and organisational breakdown in check. Douglass North defines the term 'institution' broadly to include any form of constraint that individuals devise to shape human interaction (North, 1990, p.4). Institutions include formal constraints (laws, constitutions, rules) and informal constraints (norms of behaviour, customs and conventions). Institutions are the result of cumulative learning through time, and are reflected in the ideology, beliefs, and mind set of a society. The economist's notion of a well-functioning market makes critical assumptions about the institutions that place restraints upon behaviour: '...when economists talk about efficient markets, they have simply taken for granted an elaborate framework of constraints.' (North, 1990, p.66; also see North, 1991.)[13]

In North's analysis, institutions act as the rules of the game, while organisations and entrepreneurs are some of the players (North, 1994, p.361). The incomplete nature of most contracts provides a critical rôle for informal constraints in regulating acceptable behaviour, shirking, team production, conventions, individual discretion, and so on, both within markets and within firms. Institutions play a key rôle in determining production and transaction costs at both the level of the economy and the level of the firm. Within firms rules, procedures and the organisational 'culture', reflected in the mission, help to bind people together. In a similar mode, Hayek (1960, p.27) once wrote about collective learning and the experiences passed down over time; the lessons of these experiences are embodied in our institutions, technology, language, and ways of conducting business. These background features of social order are vital to the smooth functioning of a contract-based order both outside and within firms.

The falseness of the firms-markets dichotomy suggests parallels between firms and economies. Clearly defined property rights within firms parallel property rights institutions at the economy level. Favourable incentives require the proper

---

[12] For further details see Love (1995).

[13] Another way of viewing this is to regard the institutional environment as determining the comparative costs of governance (Williamson, 1993).

specification of rights and responsibilities over outcomes within the firm through rules and operating procedures. The larger the firm, the more complex those rules and procedures tend to become. Similar to social culture (trust and norms of behaviour) is corporate culture in firms. An organisation develops its own corporate culture which constrains and shapes individual behaviour and helps determine corporate governance costs (Peters and Waterman, 1982; Casson, 1991; Johnson and Scholes, 1997).

Furthermore, organisations rely partially on trust, and not just on direct incentives, to limit opportunistic and self-seeking behaviour. Just as the government can reduce transaction costs in market economies (for example, by defining and protecting property rights) or can increase transactions costs (through bureaucracy, regulation, and red-tape), management can do so in the firm. Business firms are based on property rights, the rule of law, and trust, as are economies. Management, therefore, has the central task of introducing and maintaining the necessary institutions for well-ordered, internal-market transacting.

Contracts alone can never resolve the fundamental problems of resource allocation and production. Senior management must therefore support and encourage institutional mechanisms that help remedy the imperfections of market contracting. These mechanisms may include incentive schemes, promotion policies, corporate culture, and a firm's mission statement and 'core ideology'.[14] Management should provide a framework or environment in which internal market processes and co-operative relations can best function. Management should encourage internal markets but should also manage to prevent undue instability. Managerial direction performs a rôle similar to that performed by law-makers within the broader external market-place, and where over-manning like over-legislation leads to wasted time 'lobbying', needless uncertainty and so on.

Comparative analysis shows that only some firms have absorbed these lessons. Managers of the most successful leading-

---

[14] Prahalad and Hamel (1990, p.82) suggest that corporate success depends on 'core competence', which is 'the collective learning of the organization' about how to co-ordinate and organise work to create value. Pettigrew and Whipp (1991) talk about the 'intangible assets' of the firm. Kay talks about the firm's 'distinctive capabilities' (Kay, 1993).

edge firms typically inculcate and support a core ideology and a core set of institutional norms within their firms. Most highly successful 'visionary' firms – such as Hewlett-Packard, Nordstrom, McDonald's, Procter & Gamble, Sony and Wal-Mart – have such strong institutional norms which allow them to pursue the benefits of decentralisation without losing their coherence or a feel for their overall position in the market-place.[15]

Sometimes internal coherence is achieved by providing app-ropriate incentives for decentralised monitoring. Inform-ational burdens can prevent managers in large organisations from effectively monitoring the effort or the output of many of their workers. In such cases, economising on monitoring costs occurs through proper contract specification and the definition of rights and responsibilities in the workplace. It also occurs through the introduction and maintenance of effective operating procedures. For example, 'Just-In-Time' inventory methods coupled with 'Total Quality Management' (TQM), both popular modern management techniques, can be understood as a decentralised allocation of rights and responsibilities, in response to the dangers of chaotic decentralisation (Schonberger, 1982; Ishikawa, 1984). When properly applied, these techniques provide incentives for each group of workers to monitor and instruct the workers in the preceding production stage. They provide an in-built mode of quality control and cost management.

Traditional inventory practices can lead to the accumulation of large stocks of finished goods and components. Under Just-in-Time production, fabricated parts are supposed to arrive for use in manufacture exactly when they are needed. Workers accept the responsibility for seeing that the parts they receive contain no defects. If a problem is spotted, the production process is stopped before a large quantity of defective items is produced. Workers have an incentive to find and report defects; they wish to prevent their stage of production from being held responsible for the faulty

---

[15] Collins and Porras, in their book, *Built to Last* (1994), compare the managerial practices at Merck and at Pfizer, two large American drug companies. Merck, which has been the more successful of the two firms, has had a much stronger and more highly charged set of internal norms, geared towards a fanatical devotion to customer service. Collins and Porras note that Merck entitled its company history *Values and Visions*.

items. Furthermore, the absence of large inventories increases the cost of production hold-ups, thereby giving managers an incentive to build in quality at the earliest stages of production. In other words, 'Just-in-Time' provides an example of where monitoring becomes co-operative and decentralised, rather than the product of a hierarchical, Taylorist management. Coupled with the complementary system of TQM, the knowledge of workers on the production line is brought to bear on the quality of the product during manufacture, as in the earlier craft mode of production.[16]

The Importance of Incentives

Incentives provide the critical glue that keeps business firms co-ordinated and aimed towards a common goal. Corporations face problems of coherence when they decentralise and increase their flexibility. Managers, employees, and suppliers will not automatically choose profit-maximising courses of action, but may instead pursue their own interests or 'shirking' which conflict with the wider corporate good. The success of the firm depends, therefore, upon how well its overall corporate interest is aligned with the interests of its constituent parts. Trust, routines and the like act to create an environment conducive to the pursuit of corporate goals, but the issue of individual incentives, especially pecuniary incentives, needs further discussion.

The economic theory of incentives typically starts with the principal-agent problem, where some set of individuals (the principals) wish to have a certain task performed and an agent or agents is hired to perform that task. Usually, effort and its results will not be perfectly observable and cannot be specified fully in the contract. For example, marginal output increments may be observable after considerable time-lags, if at all. First-best contracts may, therefore, not be available and agents may

---

[16] In the Taylorist firm stock holding can be described as 'Just-In-Case': typically buffer stocks are held to aid the production flow and to meet unforeseen contingencies. For more on the link between Just-in-Time and the use of decentralised information, see Aaron (1990) and Milgrom and Roberts (1988). Just-in-Time techniques also bring other recognised benefits, such as saving money by diminishing the quantity of resources tied up in inventories, though they introduce their own risks in terms of ensuring that there are adequate supplies for the rate of production (avoiding 'stock-out').

be inclined to supply too little useful effort, especially where the principal takes the risk of the transaction not producing an economic return.

Principal-agent theory plays a rôle in most economic approaches to internal-management problems. More generally, incentive contracts form a central part of most managerial philosophies. Rather than reviewing such ideas we focus instead on how an analysis of Hayekian knowledge problems can extend and deepen our understanding of how to apply incentives. Both economics and management science often treat incentives, especially pecuniary incentives, as a static engineering problem of extracting maximum effort rather than as part of a broader programme of knowledge and discovery.

Bonuses paid by principals to agents are most effective, not only when they encourage individuals to work hard, but when they encourage the discovery and dissemination of knowledge. Too often bonus schemes encourage individuals to aggrandise their own position at the expense of the business as a whole, or at the expense of other employees. Instead, businesses should use bonuses for different purposes, including the following:

- cementing loyalty to institutions, including customs that benefit the firm as a whole;

- rewarding individuals who spread and disseminate knowledge;

- rewarding individuals who might otherwise take actions that damage the firm's interests. This includes workers who reveal that they are capable of producing more than is expected, or workers who reveal that parts of their job are superfluous and should be eliminated.

Sam Walton, former chief executive of the highly successful Wal-Mart retailing chain in the USA, had a clear understanding of the link between bonuses and knowledge problems. Walton gave department managers the freedom to run their departments like their own businesses but profitable behaviour received direct rewards. Walton created cash awards and public recognition for employees who contributed ideas for cost savings or superior service, especially if those ideas could be implemented at other stores as well. Contests were held which encouraged employees to generate new ideas. In addition to bonuses for managers, individuals at all levels of the firm participated in profit sharing and employee stock ownership. To disseminate the best new ideas, Walton even invested in a satellite communications system to spread ideas quickly throughout the company.[17]

Incentive mechanisms within firms as in external markets should act to encourage co-operative actions of individuals which achieve maximum social well-being. In particular, they must not set individuals at odds with each other.[18] Ray Kroc, the driving force behind McDonald's, recognised the importance of demonstrating co-operation with his franchisees. When Kroc ran McDonald's, most other franchisers charged high up-front fees, and took only a small percentage of the cut from the franchisee. Potentially this incentive system set franchiser and franchisee at odds. The franchiser had achieved his or her quick killing, and would not invest much in the franchise. The franchisees, in turn, felt no long-term loyalty to the franchiser, and did not act to protect the franchise name. Kroc adopted exactly the opposite strategy; he charged very small up-front franchising fees, but asked for a very high percentage of the sales, at least provided that sales reached a certain (high) level. McDonald's franchisees saw that Kroc was interested in making a long-term investment in the McDonald's brand name, which gave them confidence to invest in the franchise (Love, 1995).

Whether management should award bonuses on the basis of individual or collective performance depends upon the nature of the knowledge problem facing the firm. Collectively-based bonuses, which distribute some percentage of aggregate profits to managers and workers in the form of salary, encourage teamwork, co-operation, and identification with the

---

[17] On Walmart, see Collins and Porras (1994, pp.36-7).

[18] Although, for the sake of brevity, we concentrate upon bonuses here, similar arguments apply to other forms of incentives, including 'tournament theory' (Nalebuff and Stiglitz, 1983), which emphasises how agency costs may be reduced when employees compete for 'prizes' (such as promotion). Competition within the workforce, which is valuable in incentive terms, should not occur to the extent that individual utility is gained at the expense or well-being of the organisation as a whole.

goals of the firm. Experience indicates that collectively-based bonuses can bring significant motivational benefits. Individuals who are rewarded in accordance with the profitability of a larger business enterprise tend to identify with that enterprise to a greater degree. Each individual sees his or her fate as tied to the fate of the larger undertaking and feels part of the team. Workers are encouraged to take pride in the performance of their business enterprise and to cultivate their self-image as productive and co-operative individuals.

However, the impact on individual effort of bonuses based on aggregate profitability may be small. The effect of any single worker's productivity on aggregate profitability may be insignificant, especially in large firms. Therefore bonuses based on aggregate profitability are likely to work best in terms of stimulating effort in small firms, divisions or teams. Collectively-based bonuses have proved most effective when production is essentially a co-operative endeavour. Within many Japanese manufacturing firms, such as the automobile industry, staff work together in small teams and solve knowledge problems jointly. Senior management is greatly concerned with encouraging workers to share their local knowledge with managers, in order that assembly line techniques can be improved. In such circumstances collective bonus schemes encourage co-operative attitudes and behaviour.

'The Nordstrom Way'

The American retailer, Nordstrom, provides a good example of how individual bonuses, rather than collective bonuses, can stimulate commercial success. Nordstrom is renowned for its high levels of customer service, and treats its sales people as its primary asset. Most of the important knowledge within the company is held by the sales people, rather than the managers. The sales people are encouraged to develop ongoing, personal relationships with regular customers. It is not unusual for customers to receive personalised phone calls or notes if the store has received a new shipment of clothes, or if a sale is pending. Through such strategies, the company has developed a large and dedicated core of regular, high-income customers. The importance of individualised knowledge held by sales people is reflected in the only corporate rule that

Nordstrom has ever written; the rule reads: 'Use your good judgement in all situations. There will be no additional rules.' Nordstrom is commonly acknowledged to have the best sales help of all American departmental stores.[19]

Nordstrom gives its sales people a bonus-intensive compensation package, where bonuses are tied directly to the sales performance of the individual. Furthermore, sales people who do not meet specified targets are either fired or transferred to less important floor spaces. Sales people therefore have a maximum incentive to apply their individualised knowledge to further the success of the corporation. The customers and employees benefit from this system as well. The best Nordstrom sales people earn salaries well above US$100,000 per annum.

A comparison of the Nordstrom and Japanese bonus systems demonstrates that there is no magic formula for bonuses. Rather, incentives must be shaped to reflect the informational needs of the corporation. Unlike the Japanese employees who manufacture cars, a large proportion of Nordstrom employees come into direct contact with the firm's customers. Nordstrom sales persons apply their knowledge directly on the sales floor rather than sharing it with upper-level managers. The knowledge is unique to each customer-sales person relationship and needs to be used, not shared. Nordstrom therefore encourages competition among its sales people, rather than co-operation. The Japanese auto manufacturers, in contrast, wish to encourage co-operative rather than competitive behaviour.

Rewards encourage not only the recipient but all other workers who aspire to higher positions. The large salaries paid to many corporate executives, often criticised in the media, can motivate those employees who seek top-paying positions in the firm.[20] Many corporate executives are 'home-grown' products who have spent up to 30 years within the firm, working their way up the promotion ladder. High salaries for top positions give individuals an incentive to signal their quality to further their chances of promotion. Rather than trying to avoid monitoring, the most productive individuals actively seek out monitoring and attempt to lower its cost.

---

[19] This discussion of Nordstrom is drawn from Spector and McCarthy (1995).

[20] Crystal (1991) is an example of a polemic against high management salaries.

Market Incentives and Limits on Bonuses

Market economics does not suggest, however, the indiscriminate use of high management salaries and bonus schemes. In many instances businesses may wish to limit the direct use of pecuniary incentives for their employees. An analysis of knowledge problems provides us with clues as to when limits on bonuses may be desirable.

Despite the well-known advantages of pecuniary incentives, many businesses give them only a small place in their scheme of contracting. Some businesses have no bonus system for most of their employees, other than the binary scheme of fired/not fired. Or perhaps they have a series of pay rises or share options that vary with performance over time. Some mechanisms for raising wages place higher weight on seniority than on performance.

To some degree these organisations may be ill-informed about the beneficial aspects of market incentives. It appears, for instance, that Detroit's methods of rewarding automobile workers simply were inferior to the Japanese methods. More importantly, pecuniary incentives can sometimes backfire and lead to undesirable results. Our focus on knowledge problems within the firm helps explain why pecuniary incentives should not be used in all cases.

The mainstream perspective suggests bonuses should be eschewed when the bonus itself will skew effort towards easily measured targets, such as short-run sales or output, and away from longer-term, harder-to-measure targets, such as quality, reputation, and long-term consumer satisfaction. But there are two additional, knowledge-related reasons why bonuses are not more prevalent and should not be applied universally.

First, bonus schemes can backfire when they send negative informational feedback. Bonuses both reward individuals for creating economic value and provide information about chances of future promotion and the quality of future treatment in a firm. A low bonus may reduce effort and co-operation if an individual interprets it as a signal that his or her chances of promotion are low. Penalised individuals suddenly have less to aim for and have less reason to co-operate with other individuals in the firm. Disaffected employees tend to work very poorly and lower morale; they prove highly destructive within the organisation. If the costs of disaffected employees are higher than the motivational benefits of bonuses, the firm may be better off sending another set of informational signals – equal worth – to the relevant pool of employees.[21]

Individual bonuses work best when they interact positively rather than negatively with other incentives, such as promotion incentives. Individuals within senior management, for instance, have little further room for promotion within the company. Promotion incentives are weaker, which makes the bonus more important and decreases the likelihood that a low bonus will send a negative signal about promotion. In addition, the direct incentive effects of bonuses are usually stronger for individuals in important decision-making capacities.

Second, bonus schemes sometimes obscure information about the quality of individuals within the firm and their capabilities. When firms attempt to direct all activity with bonuses, they may lose information about how their employees will behave when no direct reward is involved, or when that employee is not being monitored.

In general, we can classify actions into those that can and those that cannot be regulated successfully with bonuses. The inability to measure accurately marginal outputs causes many actions to fall into the latter category. Given that firms cannot regulate all employee actions with bonuses, they must rely heavily on employee good will, employee concern with reputation, employee concern with the firm's customs and norms, the innate level of employee talent, and other more intangible, less directly pecuniary considerations. Employee initiative is developed by economic rewards coupled with organisational identification, including pride and loyalty (Simon, 1991).[22] Earlier in this section we referred to the rôle of institutions operating within a business firm, including the mission.

Strengthening the use of bonuses may weaken the non-bonus institutions that encourage order. Consider one possible mechanism. Firms require information about how

---

[21] For a more formal demonstration of these propositions, see Cowen and Glazer (1997). The link between promotion and bonus incentives is stressed by Gibbs (1990).

[22] The discussion has focused on rewards or 'carrots' for high performance; of course, these operate alongside the 'sticks' of reprimands, demotion and firing. Firms that rely on 'sticks' rather than 'carrots' are likely to suffer from poor staff morale and high staff turnover leading to low business performance.

employees will behave in the absence of direct pecuniary incentives. Management need to sort employees into tasks of greater and lesser responsibility, and towards that end require considerable information about employee quality. The efficiency gains of good sorting may outweigh the efficiency gains of using direct pecuniary incentives. Many employees will work hard when money is on the line, or when they are being directly observed; but which employees work hard and well all the time? Limiting the use of bonuses can generate information about employee quality and encourage the development of intra-firm institutions to regulate employee behaviour. This information can then be used to allocate individuals to their appropriate levels of responsibility and authority.

Summary

In this section we have looked in detail at some ways in which market principles may usefully be applied to improving the management of businesses. Resource allocation within the firm does not require a *fundamentally* different approach from resource allocation in markets. The firm and markets face the same economic problem of efficient resource allocation.

Organisations are complex, dynamic systems and business firms survive and prosper over time only if they are capable of responding speedily and effectively to external stimuli (Parker and Stacey, 1994). Organisations which wish to be successful must be able to assimilate, process and respond quickly to new market information and be able to stimulate individual inititiative or internal entrepreneurship. Competitive advantage will lie with those firms that can self-organise and adapt in a fashion very similar to the market economy in which they operate. Many firms are therefore abandoning the Taylorist organisation and embracing the concept of the 'learning organisation'.

Organisations involve numerous actors, each having different knowledge. Extreme centralisation is therefore one danger facing firms as it threatens the utilisation of collective knowledge. The other and opposite danger is excessive individual initiative or anarchy. The anarchic organisation is likely to lead to corporate self-destruction in double-quick time because of a lack of a coherent strategy, internal conflict over policy, and diminished financial strength. The successful organisation must promote individual and small-team working but towards a common goal.

We have seen how market principles can help in achieving this difficult balance between decentralised economic power and corporate coherence. In particular, we have reviewed how one firm, Koch Industries, uses the approach successfully. The application of market economics, involving a blend of leadership and decentralised or distributed structures, can create and maintain the appropriate balance between over-rigidity and anarchy, just as markets in an appropriate institutional context have proved successful in coping with the state of flux in the economy at large.

Markets have an ability to flex and change, assimilating and processing information speedily and accurately, attributes that are essential to the learning organisation. The alternative, a command allocation of resources, is subject to well-known inefficiencies concerned with (a) *the ability* of planners to absorb and process information in such a way as to use resources efficiently, and (b) *the incentives* within command structures for the decision-makers to use what information they have managed to gather so as to further the wider (public) interest. Indeed, the 'economics of politics' literature, which has done so much to alter economists' perceptions of government (for example, Buchanan, 1978) might usefully be applied to further understanding of *all* command structures. Firms that allocate resources by management fiat seem to be subject to the same sorts of self-seeking, pressure group actions, internal 'pork barrel' politics, budget maximisation and 'vote' winning that are the scourge of governments today.

V. CONCLUSIONS

The need for greater flexibility and fluidity in firms is placing new demands on organisational structures and processes. Firms require new ways of assimilating and adapting to complex and often confusing informational signals from the external environment. These same complexities of information, however, percolate through markets day in and day out. Markets have proved a means of handling diverse information about consumer demands and market supplies, far more effective than planning and command systems. It therefore appears paradoxical that, within market economies, large quantities of resources are allocated outside the market and within organisations.

An obvious departure point for a study of the use of market principles in managing firms is the 'markets and hierarchies' or contracts literature which examines differences and similarities between markets and firms. Given that efficient production requires the existence of firms, to what extent can market principles guide resource allocation within them? Or to put this in another way, what is the potential rôle for market methods in firms which appear at present to have many of the attributes of a planned economy?

An Enhanced Rôle for Economics

Neo-Walrasian general equilibrium analysis plays a large rôle in contemporary micro-economics. It is principally concerned with the conditions under which markets clear, leaving no excess supply or demand. Partial imperfections or quantity-constrained markets have been introduced into the theory, but the prevailing emphasis remains one of perfect co-ordination, given the initial constraints. Mathematically neat, the theory has fascinated generations of economists since it was formalised by Leon Walras in the late-19th century. Economists like the theory because it provides 'exact' conditions for the perfect co-ordination of individual economic activities.

This theoretical exactness, however, assumes away many of the important issues involved in the practical co-ordination of economic activity. Even in its more advanced formulations, deriving from the models of Arrow, Debreu, and Hahn, competitive equilibrium theory does not remotely resemble real-world markets (Clower, 1994, p.809). In particular, in a Walrasian world co-ordination of the decisions of a multitude of economic agents is cost free. Market exchanges occur in a frictionless fashion, unencumbered by the practical problems of seeking out consumers and suppliers, arranging contracts and monitoring and policing them. Indeed, there is no market trading as such but only a series of pre-arranged transactions struck at the first moment of economic time. Markets that move automatically to an equilibrium remove any rationale for strategic decision-making. In this theory nothing remotely resembling a real firm exists *or can exist.*

For many years the considerable investment of intellectual effort in general equilibrium theory diverted attention away from studying the market as a process of information generation and transmission. In most formulations of general equilibrium theory information is complete or uncertainty exists only in a well-defined, probabilistic sense. But real-world markets are concerned with *discovering* that information which Walrasian analysis takes as a given.

Similarly, in much of neo-classical analysis, heavily influenced by Walrasian analysis, the firm is largely an assumption introduced into stylistic models of competitive and imperfectly competitive markets. By implication, the firm is often equated with the single entrepreneur, in the sense that 'the firm' is said to set price and output. But entrepreneurship has no rôle because information is assumed to be either complete or probabilistically complete. If information is complete then no person can have superior information to another person and there is no potential for enterprise, for there is nothing useful to discover about consumers or inputs. No person can make more (risk-adjusted) profit than another person by obtaining better information about consumer wants or by better employing factors of production. The entrepreneurial function disappears without trace.[1] With the engine of the market economy removed, the remaining theoretical construct can hardly be called a market economy.

---

[1] For a review of the neglect of enterprise in economic theorising, see Parker and Stead (1991). Also see Israel Kirzner (1997).

That the neo-classical 'theory of the firm' is not a theory of the firm at all but rather a theory of perfectly competitive markets, is now well recognised. In this theory the firm is a 'black box' or void in which inputs are (somehow) frictionlessly converted into outputs. The theory does not address how these inputs are converted and under what decision-making process; instead, market participants react automatically and reliably to all price signals.

In reality the notion that a 'firm' produces and prices outputs is misleading. Firms are inanimate constructs and cannot produce anything without human action. Only individuals working within the firm and using its capital stock and material inputs can produce outputs. However, once we introduce the notion of individuals producing, then decision-taking becomes of central importance to economists; the firm ceases to be a black box and instead becomes a primary focus of economic study.

The neo-classical treatment of the firm as a black box, at least until the last two decades or so, has left the study of internal structures and processes largely to others.[2] As a result the strategic management and organisational theory literatures have developed separately from economics. Indeed, today management theorists and economists often occupy separate departments (and sometimes separate faculties) within universities. But this separation was not always so, nor was it inevitable. A century ago economists were centrally concerned with the operation of business, as illustrated in the writings of Alfred Marshall. Marshall wrote about businesses using analogies of firms with biological processes of birth, growth, maturity, decay and death – ideas that remain relevant to modern business organisations.[3]

---

[2] Simon (1957) and Cyert and March (1963) are well known for their attempts to open up the black box using a behaviouralist perspective. From that perspective firms consist of individuals and coalitions, and organisational goals result from continuous intra-firm bargaining. But, as Bianchi (1990) points out, what is missing from such behavioural theory is the notion of decision-making as a learning process.

[3] Although much more attention is now paid to the firm in economics (see Section III) it is still true that in the economics literature much more interest is shown in the economics of industrial organisation than in the economics of the firm.

The division between business or management studies and economics has left much of economics isolated from the study of resource allocation by management.[4] Equally worrying has been the tendency of both management theorists and management practitioners to question the value of an understanding of micro-economics to the running of a business. For example, a number of MBA courses, the primary post-graduate business qualification, have no micro-economics in their course structure. Others have a mere smattering. Few if any contain a detailed study of micro-economic principles to an advanced level. The same is true of senior manager courses at many leading business schools.

Perhaps of most immediate worry for the future of economic studies in the UK has been the sudden collapse in demand to study economics by school pupils in favour of courses in 'business studies'.[5] There are signs of similar trends at undergraduate level. The reintroduction of economic principles into the study of resource allocation within firms offers a valuable opportunity to stem the decline of economic studies. We have endeavoured to show how a knowledge of market principles can be the basis for the understanding and further study of business. Even some of the most basic micro-economic concepts can be utilised to develop understanding of the organisation. An economics that re-emphasises the rôle of micro-economics in business organisation and 'strategic management' should also provide a basis for reversing the current decline of economic study within schools and universities. Market economics can be a solution not only to management problems but to the decline of the study of economics in educational institutions.

Market Principles and the Firm

This *Hobart Paper* has attempted to demonstrate how, through an understanding of the economics of transaction costs and a broader application of market principles to the study of

---

4 For an interesting discussion of the separation of economics from business and what might be done, see Kay (1991).

5 *Editor's note:* In Economics the number of GCE A/AS Level passes has fallen from 23,700 in 1991/92 to 15,100 in 1995/96: in Business Studies the number of passes increased from 12,200 to 17,600 over the same period (Department for Education and Employment).

77

resource allocation within organisations, firms can innovate so as to achieve greater competitive advantage. This is no mean achievement. It may fall short of the revolution in ownership for which some people hanker, but it should meet the aspirations of the vast majority who want to improve the efficiency of their businesses.

The alternative to the use of market principles within firms is a continuation of the command-and-control or Taylorist paradigm. But the command firm is subject to all the disincentives of planned economies, including the hiding of resources, aggravated shortages, the over- or under-use of inputs and the resulting inefficiencies in production.

Whereas the Taylorist firm may have been well suited to economic conditions earlier this century, the need for greater flexibility and adaptability to compete successfully requires a new and leaner 'learning organisation' which can successfully seek out and profitably use the vast flow of information in the modern economy. Too often the long and narrow management channel in command firms leads to new ideas being cut off before they reach board level. Moreover, in these organisations independent thinking is discouraged in favour of conformance to organisational rules and procedures. Competitive advantage depends upon information and knowledge and, as Hayek and others pointed out earlier this century, planners inevitably lack the information and knowledge to allocate resources efficiently. In short, today organisations need to self-organise and adapt to mimic markets in discovering and mobilising dispersed information.

A company that promotes multiple sources of decision-making gains competitive advantage by tapping *all* of the abilities within the firm. Humans differ in their knowledge, skills, capabilities and attitudes, and this rich heterogeneity is an economy's most valuable resource. The successful firm is one that can tap into this resource, producing the internal experimentation and discovery processes upon which true entrepreneurship is built.[6] Experimentation has been identified as the key factor in the success of Western capitalism (Rosenberg, 1994, p.99). The firm that successfully adapts

---

[6] The argument here is similar to that in Richardson (1960 and 1972) that, in essence, a firm is a set of capabilities and the firm makes most profit by specialising in those capabilities.

market principles to guide internal resource allocation will be able to remove more of the centralised command-and-control mechanism that stultifies entrepreneurial responses to changes in the external environment. In essence, therefore, what is needed (and what is happening) is the replacement of the command-and-control form of organisation with a looser structure that promotes experimentation. But the loosely coupled organisation is something with which most managers are uncomfortable; giving up the levers of command and control is contrary to their experience. Loose coupling also brings real risks in the form of organisational anarchy and breakdown.

We have argued in this *Hobart Paper* that price signals provide both the information and the incentives that reduce the need for command and centralised direction within the firm. As Armen Alchian observed (Alchian, 1950), economic evolution or change is best achieved where there is decentralised decision-making which provides for the numerous trials or experiments needed to discover the best ways of solving economic problems.

An application of market principles to management emphasises three essential economic features:

- the discovery, dissemination and integration of knowledge within the firm;

- the importance of clear property rights and responsibilities within the firm; and

- the use of appropriate incentives at all levels of production and decision-making (Cowen and Ellig, 1995, p.2).

This approach is consistent with the changing needs of businesses as they accommodate to the rapid pace of economic and social change and the resulting flows of information. It is consistent also with the economics literature on transaction cost economics and contracting in firms and markets (Section III).

The goal should not necessarily be to push decisions down to the ranks (the possible result of a blind pursuit of 'empowerment' and 'delayering'), but to put the decision-making in the hands of persons or teams with the best ability to maximise the use of the firm's scarce resources. In other words, the rôle of 'top' management should be to institute processes or procedures that enable resources to be distributed in such a way as to maximise the productivity and profitability of the firm. Market economies have proved effective in encouraging learning, adaptation and innovation. The challenge today is to design firms that can mimic these attributes of the market economy. Command economies have shown themselves inferior in terms of absorbing and processing information and reacting to changing consumer needs; they also provide insufficient incentives to economise on resource use and operate efficiently. By contrast, the greatest attribute of the decentralised market economy is that it permits decentralised decision-making, which in turn allows numerous trials or experiments to discover the best way of solving economic problems over time.

This paper has considered some general principles which are a guide to how market economics can aid management. Future research needs to focus on the internal and institutional impediments to the use of these principles. One particular area that needs exploring is current accounting practices. The development of 'activity-based accounting' appears to be a step in the right direction by allocating joint costs or overheads more effectively so as to identify the true costs of production in various parts of the firm. Another area is the application of market principles to the management of not-for-profit firms. To what extent do the principles developed in this paper need to be modified if they are to be applied in firms which do not have a profit motive (including government departments and agencies)?

A decentralised outcome results from the use of tacit knowledge and therefore creative entrepreneurship (North, 1990, p.81). As Western firms face increased global competition and as the Taylorist firm becomes less relevant, market principles offer a means of maximising individual performance without losing the collective, strategic direction that defines the successful firm. History shows that free markets promote individual discovery, innovation and high productivity. They are a means to realise every individual's potential contribution to economic well-being. They are as effective within organisations as without.

TOPICS/QUESTIONS FOR DISCUSSION

1. What are the implications of market economics for the management of business firms?

2. Do the economics of firms and the economics of markets differ in kind, or are they fundamentally similar?

3. How have the economics of production and business management changed over the last two centuries?

4. What are the implications of the Hayekian discovery process for management?

5. What are the rôles of enterprise and management in a business firm?

6. What can management do to prevent decentralisation from collapsing into organisational anarchy?

7. How should business incentives be structured to reflect the importance of information and discovery?

8. How does the topic of non-linear dynamics relate to the use of market economics for management?

9. In what ways are traditional management theories deficient?

10. In what ways do many traditional management methods suffer from the defects of central planning?

REFERENCES/BIBLIOGRAPHY

Aaron, D.J. (1990): 'Firm Organization and the Economic Approach to Personnel Management', *American Economic Review*, May, pp.23-27.

Alchian, A. A. (1950): 'Uncertainty, evolution and economic theory', *Journal of Political Economy*, Vol. 58.

Alchian, A.A. and Demsetz, H. (1972): 'Production, Information Costs and Economic Organization', *American Economic Review*, Vol.62, No.5, pp.777-95.

Arrow, K.J. (1969): 'The Organization of Economic Activity: issues pertinent to the choice of market versus nonmarket allocation', in *Joint Economic Committee, The Analysis and Evolution of Public Expenditure: the PPB System, Vol.1*, Washington DC.: US Government Printing Office.

Arrow, K.J. (1974): *The Limits of Organization*, New York: Norton.

Ashby, W.R. (1956): *Introduction to Cybernetics*, New York: John Wiley.

Atkinson, J. and Meager, N. (1986): *Changing Work Patterns: How Companies Achieve Flexibility to Meet New Needs*, London: National Economic Development Office.

Badaracco, J. L. Jnr. (1987): 'The New General Motors', *Harvard Business School Case Study*.

Bartlett, C. and Ghoshal, S. (1989): *Managing Across Borders: The Transnational Solution*, Boston, Mass.: Harvard Business School Press.

Bartlett, C. and Ghoshal, S. (1990): 'Matrix Management: Not a Structure but a Frame of Mind', *Harvard Business Review*, Vol.68, No.4, pp.138-45.

Barzel, Y. (1982): 'Measurement Cost and the Organization of Markets', *Journal of Law and Economics*, Vol.25, pp.27-48.

Berle, A.A. and Means, G.C. (1933): *The Modern Corporation and Private Property*, New York: Macmillan.

Bianchi, M. (1990): 'The Unsatisfactoriness of Satisficing: from bounded rationality to innovative rationality', *Review of Political Economy*, Vol.2, pp.149-67.

Boettke, P. (1990): *The Political Economy of Soviet Socialism*, Boston: Kluwer Academic Publishers.

Boisot, M. (1995): *Information Space: a Framework for Learning in Organizations, Institutions and Culture*, London: Routledge.

Brickley, J.A., Smith, C.W. and Zimmerman, J.L. (1997): *Managerial Economics and Organizational Architecture*, Chicago: Irwin.

Buchanan, J. (ed.) (1978): *The Economics of Politics*, IEA Readings No. 18, London: Institute of Economic Affairs.

Buckley, P.J. (1983): 'New Theories of International Business: some unresolved problems', in M. Casson (ed.), *The Growth of International Business*, London: Allen & Unwin.

Buckley, P.J. (1988): 'The Limits of Explanation – testing the international theory of multinational enterprise', *Journal of International Business Studies*, Vol.19, pp.181-93.

Buckley, P.J. and Casson, M. (1976): *The Future of the Multinational Enterprise*, London: Macmillan.

Burgoyne, J.G. (1992): 'Creating a Learning Organization', *RSA Journal*, Vol. CXI, pp.321-32.

Burton, J. (1996): 'Composite Strategy: the Combination of Collaboration and Competition', *Journal of General Management*, Vol.21, No.1, pp.1-21.

Casson, M. (1982): *The Entrepreneur: an economic theory*, Oxford: Blackwell.

Casson, M. (1991): *The Economics of Business Culture*, Oxford: Clarendon Press.

Casson, M. (1994): 'Why are Firms Hierarchical?', *Journal of the Economics of Business*, Vol.1, No.1, pp.47-76.

Caulkin, S. (1995): 'The Pursuit of Immortality', *Management Today*, May, pp.36-40.

Chandler, A.D. (1962): *Strategy and Structure*, Cambridge, Mass.: MIT Press.

Chandler, A.D. (1977): *The Visible Hand: the Managerial Revolution in American Business*, Cambridge, Mass.: Harvard University Press.

Chandler, A.D. (1990): *Scale and Scope: the Dynamics of Industrial Capitalism*, Cambridge, Mass.: Harvard University Press.

Cheung, S.N.S. (1983): 'The Contractual Nature of the Firm', *Journal of Law and Economics*, April, pp.1-21.

Clower, R.W. (1994): 'Economics as an Inductive Science', *Southern Economic Journal*, Vol.60, No.4, pp.805-14.

Coase, R.H. (1937): 'The Nature of the Firm', *Economica*, Vol.4, pp.386-405; reprinted in O.E. Williamson and S.G. Winter (eds.), *The Nature of the Firm: Origins, Evolution and Development*, Oxford: Oxford University Press.

Coase, R. H. (1960): 'The Problem of Social Cost', in *Journal of Law and Economics*, Vol. 3, October.

Coase, R.H. (1991a): 'The Nature of the Firm: Origins', in O.E. Williamson and S.G. Winter (eds.), *The Nature of the Firm: Origins, Evolution and Development*, Oxford: Oxford University Press.

Coase, R.H. (1991b): 'The Nature of the Firm: Meaning', in O.E. Williamson and S.G. Winter (eds.), *The Nature of the Firm: Origins, Evolution and Development*, Oxford: Oxford University Press.

Collins, J.C. and Porras, J.I. (1994): *Built to Last: Successful Habits of Visionary Companies*, New York: Harper Business.

Cowen, T. and Ellig, J. (1995): 'Market-Based Management at Koch Industries: Discovery, Dissemination, and Integration of Knowledge', *Competitive Intelligence Review*, Vol.6, No.4, pp.4-13.

Cowen, T. and Glazer, A. (1997): 'Imperfect Information May Alleviate Agency Problems', *Journal of Economic Behavior and Organization* (forthcoming).

Cowling, K. and Sugden, R. (1994): 'The Essence of the Modern Corporation: Markets, Strategic Decision-Making and the Theory of the Firm', *Occasional Papers in Industrial Strategy No.34*, Research Centre for Industrial Strategy, University of Birmingham.

Crystal, G. S. (1991): *In Search of Excess: the Overcompensation of American Executives*, New York: Norton and Co.

Cyert, R.M. and March, J.G. (1963): *A Behavioral Theory of the Firm*, Englewood Cliffs, NJ: Prentice Hall.

Department for Education and Employment, *GCE A/AS Attempts and Passes of Pupils in all Schools and Higher Education Colleges*, 1991/92 to 1995/96.

Deming, W. E. (1982): *Quality, Productivity and Competitive Position*, Mass.: MIT Centre for Advanced Engineering Study.

Deming, W. E. (1988): *Out of the Crisis*, Cambridge: Cambridge University Press.

Dietrich, M. (1994): *Transaction Cost Economics and Beyond: towards a new economics of the firm*, London: Routledge.

Drucker, P. (1992): 'The Coming of the New Organisation', in G. Salaman (ed.), *Human Resource Strategies*, London: Sage.

Drucker, P. (1993): *Post-Capitalist Society*, Oxford: Butterworth Heinemann.

Eccles, R. (1985): *The Transfer Pricing Problem: a Theory for Practice*, Lexington, Mass.: Lexington Books.

Economist, 10 June 1995, p. 79.

Economist, 'The outing of outsourcing', 2 November 1995, pp.99-100.

Economist, 'A Survey of Business in Asia', 9 March 1996, supplement.

Ellig, J. (1993): 'Internal Pricing for Corporate Services', *Working Paper in Market-Based Management*, Centre for the Study of Market Processes, George Mason University.

Fama, E.F. (1980): 'Agency Problems and the Theory of the Firm'. *Journal of Political Economy*, Vol.88, pp.288-307.

85

Fama, E.F. and Jensen, M.C. (1983): 'Separation of Ownership and Control', *Journal of Law and Economics*, Vol.26, pp.301-25.

Financial Times, P. Martin, 'In, out and shake it all about', 16 May 1996, p.22.

Financial Times, L. Bilmes, 'The seedbed of job creation', 10 June 1996, p.10.

Financial Times, S. Wagstyl, 'An open market in industrial research', 22 October 1996, p.14.

Fox, A. (1974): *Beyond Contract: work, power and trust relations*, London: Faber & Faber.

Friedman, M. (1953): 'The Methodology of positive economics', in M. Friedman, *Essays in Positive Economics*, Chicago: University of Chicago Press.

Gable, W. and Ellig, J. (1993): *Introduction to Market-Based Management*, Foreword by C.G. Koch, Center for the Study of Market Processes, George Mason University, Fairfax, Virginia.

Gibbs, M. J. (1990): *Assignment, Information and Incentives: an Economic Approach to Process in Pay and Performance Appraisals*, Harvard Business School Working Paper.

Goold, M. and Campbell, A. (1987): *Strategies and Styles: the Rôle of the Centre*, Oxford: Basil Blackwell.

Grossman, S. and Hart, O. (1986): 'The Costs and Benefits of Ownership: a theory of vertical and lateral integration', *Journal of Political Economy*, Vol.94, pp.691-719.

Halal, W., Geranmayeh, A. and Pourdehnad, J. (1993): *Internal Markets: Bringing the Power of Free Enterprise Inside your Organization*, New York: Wiley.

Handy, C. (1994): *The Empty Raincoat: Making Sense of the Future*, Hutchinson: London.

Hayek, F.A. (1945): 'The Use of Knowledge in Society', *American Economic Review*, Vol.35, pp.519-30.

Hayek, F.A. (1948): *Individualism and Economic Order*, Chicago: University of Chicago Press.

Hayek, F.A. (1960): *The Constitution of Liberty*, London: Routledge & Kegan Paul.

Hayek, F.A. (1978): *New Studies in Philosophy, Politics, Economics and the History of Ideas*, London: Routledge & Kegan Paul.

Hennart, J.F. (1991a): 'Control in Multinational Firms: the Rôle of Price and Hierarchy', *Management International Review*, special issue, pp.71-96.

Hennart, J.F. (1991b): 'The Transaction Cost Theory of Multinational Enterprise', in C. Pitelis and R. Sugden (eds.), *The Nature of the Transnational Firm*, London: Routledge.

Hirst, P. and Zeitlin, J. (1989): 'Flexible Specialisation and the Competitive Failure of UK Manufacturing', *Political Quarterly*, Vol.60, pp.164-78.

Hodgson, G. (1993): 'Transaction Costs and the Evolution of the Firm', in C. Pitelis (ed.), *Transaction Costs, Markets and Hierarchies*, Oxford: Blackwell.

Ingrassia, P. and White, J.B. (1994): *Comeback: The Fall and Rise of the American Automobile Industry*, New York: Simon and Schuster, 1994.

Ishikawa, K. (1984): 'Quality Production in Japan', in N. Sasaki and D. Hutchins (eds.), *The Japanese Approach to Product Quality*, London: Pergamon.

Jensen, M.C. and Meckling, W.H. (1976): 'The Theory of the Firm: managerial behavior, agency costs and ownership structure', *Journal of Financial Economics*, Vol.3, pp.305-60.

Johnson, G. and Scholes, K. (1997): *Exploring Corporate Strategy: Text and Cases*, 4th edition, London: Prentice Hall.

Kakabadse, A. (1991): *The Wealth Creators: Top People, Top Teams & Executive Best Practice*, London: Kogan Page.

Kanter, R.M. (1990): *When Giants Learn to Dance*, London: Unwin.

Kay, J.A. (1991): 'Economics and Business', *Economic Journal*, Vol.101, January, pp.57-63.

Kay, J.A. (1993): *Foundations of Corporate Success: How Business Strategies Add Value*, Oxford: Oxford University Press.

Kirzner, I.M. (1985): *Discovery and the Capitalist Process*, Chicago: University of Chicago Press.

Kirzner, I.M. (1997): *How Markets Work: Disequilibrium, Entrepreneurship and Discovery*, IEA Hobart Paper 133, London: Institute of Economic Affairs.

Klein, R. (1983): 'Contracting Costs and Residual Claims: the Separation of Ownership and Control', *Journal of Law and Economics*, Vol.26, No.2, pp.367-74.

Klein, B., Crawford, R.G. and Alchian, A.A. (1978): 'Vertical Integration, Appropriable Rents and Competitive Contracting Process', *Journal of Law and Economics*, Vol.21, pp.297-326.

Knight, F.H. (1921): *Risk, Uncertainty and Profit*, New York: Harper & Row, 1965.

Langlois, R.N. (1984): 'International Organization in a Dynamic Context: some theoretical considerations', in M. Jussawalla and H. Ebenfield (eds.), *Communication and Information Economics: New Perspectives*, Amsterdam: North-Holland.

Leonard-Barton, D. (1995): *Wellsprings of Knowledge: Building and Sustaining the Sources of Innovation*, Cambridge, Mass.: Harvard Business School Press.

Love, J.F. (1995): *McDonald's: Behind the Arches*, New York: Bantam Books.

Machlup, F. (1967): 'Theories of the Firm: Marginalist, Behavioral and Managerial', *American Economic Review*, Vol.57, pp.1-83.

Management Today, 'Barclays finds healthy interest in its IT expertise', March 1996.

Mann, N.R. (1989): *The Keys to Excellence: the Story of the Deming Philosophy*, Los Angeles: Prestwick Books.

Marglin, S.A. (1974): '"What Do Bosses Do?" The origins and function of hierarchy in capitalist production', *Review of Radical Political Economics*, Vol.6, pp.60-112.

Marschak, J. and Radner, R. (1972): *Economic Theory of Teams*, New Haven, CT: Yale University Press.

Matsushita, K. (1988): 'The Secret is Shared', *Manufacturing Economics*, February, p.15.

Milgrom, P. and Roberts, J. (1988): 'Communication and Inventory as Substitutes in Organizing Production', *Scandinavian Journal of Economics*, Vol. 90, pp.275-89.

Milgrom, P. and Roberts, J. (1992): *Economics, Organization and Management*, Englewood Cliffs, NJ: Prentice Hall.

Moss Kanter, R. (1983): *The Change Masters: Corporate Entrepreneurs at Work*, London: Unwin.

Nalebuff, B. and Stiglitz, J. (1983): 'Prizes and Incentives: Towards a General Theory of Compensation and Competition', *Bell Journal of Economics*, Vol.13, pp.21-43.

Nelson, R.R. and Winter, S.G. (1982): *The Evolutionary Theory of Economic Change*, Boston, Mass.: Harvard University Press.

North, D.C. (1990): *Institutions, Institutional Change and Economic Performance*, Cambridge: Cambridge University Press.

North, D.C. (1991): 'Institutions', *Journal of Economic Perspectives*, Vol.5, Winter, pp.97-112.

North, D.C. (1994): 'Economic Performance through Time', *American Economic Review*, Vol.84, No.3, June, pp.359-68.

Ouchi, W.G. (1980): 'Markets, Bureaucracies and Clans', *Administrative Science Quarterly*, Vol.25, pp.129-41.

Parker, D. and Stead, R. (1991): *Profit and Enterprise: The Political Economy of Profit*, London: Harvester Wheatsheaf; New York: St Martin's Press.

Parker, D. and Stacey, R. (1994): *Chaos, Management and Economics: the implications of non-linear thinking*, IEA Hobart Paper 125, London: Institute of Economic Affairs.

Parker, D. and Hartley, K. (1996): 'The Economics of Partnership Sourcing versus Adversarial Competition: a critique', *Department of Commerce Working Paper*, University of Birmingham.

Penrose, E. (1995): *The Theory of the Growth of the Firm*, 3rd edition, Oxford: Oxford University Press.

Person, H.S. (1929): 'The Origin and Nature of Scientific Management', in H.S. Person (ed.), *Scientific Management in American Industry*, New York & London: Harper & Brothers.

Peters, T. (1987): *Thriving on Chaos*, London: Macmillan.

Peters, T. and Waterman, R.H. (1982): *In Search of Excellence*, New York: Harper & Row.

Pettigrew, A. and Whipp, R. (1991): *Managing Change for Competitive Success*, Oxford: Blackwell.

Pitelis, C. (ed.) (1993): *Transaction Costs, Markets and Hierarchies*, Oxford: Blackwell.

Polanyi, M. (1951): *The Logic of Liberty: Reflections and Rejoinders*, Chicago: University of Chicago Press.

Porter, M.E. (1985): *Competitive Advantage: Creating and Sustaining Superior Performance*, New York: Free Press.

Prahalad, C.K. and Hamel, G. (1990): 'The Core Competence of the Corporation', *Harvard Business Review*, May-June, pp.79-91.

Putterman, L. (1984): 'On Some Recent Explanations of Why Capital Hires Labour', *Economic Inquiry*, Vol.12, pp.171-87.

Richardson, G.B. (1960; reprinted 1990): *Information and Investment: a Study in the Working of the Competitive Economy*, Oxford: Oxford University Press.

Richardson, G.B. (1972): 'The Organization of Industry', *Economic Journal*, Vol.82, September, pp.882-96.

Ricketts, M. (1994): *The Economics of Business Enterprise*, 2nd edition, London: Harvester Wheatsheaf.

Robertson, I. (1995): in R. Lamming and A. Cox (eds.), *Strategic Procurement Management in the 1990s*, The Chartered Institute of Purchasing and Supply, London: Earlsgate Press.

Rosenberg, N. (1994): *Exploring the Black Box: Technology, Economics and History*, Cambridge: Cambridge University Press.

Sampson, A. (1995): *Company Man: The Rise and Fall of Corporate Life*, London: HarperCollins.

Schonberger, R. (1982): *Japanese Manufacturing Techniques*, New York: Free Press.

Schumpeter, J. (1934): *The Theory of Economic Development: An Inquiry into Profits, Capital, Credit, Interest, and the Business Cycle*, Cambridge, Mass.: Harvard University Press.

Senge, P.E. (1993): *The Fifth Discipline: The Art and Practice of the Learning Organisation*, London: Century Business.

Simon, H.A. (1957): *Models of Man: Social and Rational*, London: John Wiley.

Simon, H.A. (1972): 'Theories of Bounded Rationality', in C.McGuire and R.Radner (eds.), *Decision and Organization*, Amsterdam: North-Holland.

Simon, H.A. (1991): 'Organizations and Markets', *Journal of Economic Perspectives*, Vol.5, No.2, pp.25-44.

Spector, R. and McCarthy, P.D. (1995): *The Nordstrom Way: The Inside Story of America's #1 Customer Service Company*, New York: John Wiley & Sons.

Taylor, F.W. (1911): *Principles of Scientific Management*, New York: Norton.

Tiernan, S. (1993): 'Innovations in Organisational Structure', *Irish Business and Administration Research*, Vol.14, No.2, pp.57-68.

Tirole, J. (1986): 'Hierarchies and Bureaucracy: On the Rôle of Collusion in Organizations', *Journal of Law, Economics and Organization*, Vol.2, pp.181-214.

Vancil, R. (1978): *Decentralisation: Managerial Ambiguity by Design*, New York: Dow Jones-Irwin.

Wall Street Journal, 'Charles Koch teaches his staff to run firm like a free nation', 18 April 1997.

Weber, M. (1948; 1970 edition): *Essays in Sociology*, London: Routledge & Kegan Paul.

Williamson, O.E. (1975): *Markets and Hierarchies: Analysis and Anti-trust Implications*, New York: Free Press.

Williamson, O.E. (1985): *The Economic Institutions of Capitalism: Firms, Markets, and History,* Cambridge: Cambridge University Press.

Williamson, O.E. (1991): 'The Logic of Economic Organization', in O.E. Williamson and S.G. Winter (eds.), *The Nature of the Firm: Origins, Evolution and Development,* Oxford: Oxford University Press.

Williamson, O.E. (1993): 'Transaction Cost Economics and Organization Theory', *Journal of Industrial and Corporate Change,* Vol.2, pp.107-56.

Willman, P. (1983): 'The Organisational Failures Framework and Industrial Sociology', in A. Francis, J. Turk and P. Willman (eds.), *Power, Efficiency and Institutions,* London: Heinemann.

Womack, J., Jones, D. and Ross, D. (1990): *The Machine that Changed the World,* New York: HarperCollins.

Chaos, Management and Economics

The Implications of Non-Linear Thinking

David Parker & Ralph Stacey

1. Chaos theory, which is causing a revolution in the natural sciences, has important lessons for the study of how human organisations and economies function.

2. Chaos is an 'intricate mixture of order and disorder' in which behaviour patterns are irregular. Nevertheless, broad categories of behaviour can be recognised.

3. Links between causes and effects are more complex than simple linear systems can capture.

4. The behaviour of any system may well be extremely sensitive to its 'initial conditions'. Such systems cannot be controlled; they 'evolve through a process of self-organisation'.

5. Because the long-term future is unknowable, managements of both companies and economies should emphasise adaptability and creativeness.

6. Competitive markets are vital to the creative process because, unlike planned systems, they provide for 'spontaneous adaptation'.

7. Enterprise is a 'locomotive of change'. Chaos theory 'provides a new argument for the innovating entrepreneur' which complements the case made by the Austrian school. To cope with chaotic conditions, economies need to promote entrepreneurship.

8. In chaotic conditions, slight errors in demand management may lead to increased economic instability.

9. Companies and economies '...require structures and institutions which encourage self-transformation', not detailed plans for long-term futures.

10. Government economic and social policy should '...complement not conflict with economic change', avoiding policies which '...reduce the economy's ability to adapt, including regulation, monopoly and high taxation...'.

The Institute of Economic Affairs

2 Lord North Street, Westminster, London SW1P 3LB
Telephone: 0171 799 3745 Facsimile: 0171 799 2137
E-mail: iea@iea.org.uk Internet: http://www.iea.org.uk   ISBN 0-255 36333-8

£9.00

Back From the Brink: An Appeal to Fellow Europeans Over Monetary Union

Pedro Schwartz

1. European Monetary Union is an 'unprecedented experiment', a 'huge gamble' which produces mixed reactions among Europeans.

2. There are many possible pitfalls before monetary union can come into being. One particular problem is that from 1998 to 2001, national currencies will remain legal tender. The currencies of 'misbehaving countries' may therefore be '…pounced upon by speculators and marauders…'

3. A monetary zone can function effectively only if it encompasses a single market, especially a single labour market. Establishing a monetary union when there is no hope of removing some of the barriers to a single market means '…applying perpetual fetters'.

4. The labour market of the European Union is '…far from being integrated'. The entry into monetary union of countries with rigid labour markets would warp the functioning of the union: moreover, those countries would probably demand subsidies to alleviate unemployment.

5. European Monetary Union therefore faces 'a bumpy road' before and after 2002. Before 2002 there may be 'speculative storms'; after 2002 large pockets of unemployment may persist, undermining European unity.

6. If European politicians had really wanted a stable currency they would have linked their currencies to the Deutschmark and turned their Central Banks into currency boards.

7. Monetary competition among existing European currencies plus the euro would offer a better long run prospect of monetary stability than monetary union.

8. Competitive devaluation is less of a problem than industrial lobbies claim. Over-valuation is more of a danger: '…fake converts from easy virtue love the prestige of a strong currency'.

9. In practice, careful economic analysis of European Monetary Union 'counts for nothing'. The proposed union is a 'dangerous experiment…' to build a certain kind of Europe surreptitiously' and to give a '…huge boost to centralisation'.

10. If monetary union goes ahead, Britain should go it alone and '…set an example from within the European Union of what can be achieved by a competitive, deregulated, private economy with a floating and well-managed currency'.

The Institute of Economic Affairs

2 Lord North Street, Westminster, London SW1P 3LB
Telephone: 0171 799 3745 Facsimile: 0171 799 2137
E-mail: iea@iea.org.uk Internet: http://www.iea.org.uk   ISBN 0-255 36401-6

£4.00

Less Than Zero

The Case for a Falling Price Level in a Growing Economy

George Selgin

1. Most economists now accept that monetary policy should not aim at 'full employment': central banks should aim instead at limiting movements in the general price level.

2. Zero inflation is often viewed as an ideal. But there is a case for allowing the price level to vary so as to reflect changes in unit production costs.

3. Under such a 'productivity norm', monetary policy would allow 'permanent improvements in productivity…to lower prices permanently' and adverse supply shocks (such as wars and failed harvests) to bring about temporary price increases. The overall result would be '…secular deflation interrupted by occasional negative supply shocks'.

4. United States consumer prices would have halved in the 30 years after the Second World War (instead of almost tripling), had a productivity norm policy been in operation.

5. In an economy with rising productivity a constant price level cannot be relied upon to avoid '…"unnatural" fluctuations in output and employment'.

6. A productivity norm should involve lower 'menu' costs of price adjustment, minimise 'monetary misperception' effects, achieve more efficient outcomes using fixed money contracts and keep the real money stock closer to its 'optimum'.

7. The theory supporting the productivity norm runs counter to conventional macro-economic wisdom. For example, it suggests that a falling price level is not synonymous with depression. The 'Great Depression' of 1873-1896 was actually a period of '…unprecedented advances in factor productivity'.

8. In practice, implementing a productivity norm would mean choosing between a labour productivity and a total factor productivity norm. Using the latter might be preferable and would involve setting the growth rate of nominal income equal to a weighted average of labour and capital input growth rates.

9. Achieving a predetermined growth rate of nominal income would be easier under a free banking régime which tends automatically to stabilise nominal income.

10. Many countries now have inflation rates not too far from zero. But zero inflation should be recognised not as the ideal but '…as the stepping-stone towards something even better'.

The Institute of Economic Affairs

2 Lord North Street, Westminster, London SW1P 3LB
Telephone: 0171 799 3745 Facsimile: 0171 799 2137
E-mail: iea@iea.org.uk Internet: http://www.iea.org.uk   ISBN 0-255 36402-4

£8.00

How Markets Work:
Disequilibrium, Entrepreneurship and Discovery

Israel M. Kirzner

1. Mainstream neo-classical economics focusses on already attained states of equilibrium. It is silent about the processes of adjustment to equilibrium.

2. Human action consists of '...grappling with an essentially unknown future', not being confronted with clearly-specified objectives, known resources and defined courses of action as mainstream theory assumes.

3. Critics of the market economy find ammunition in neo-classical theory: they '...merely need to tick off the respects in which real world capitalism departs from the requirements for perfectly competitive optimality'.

4. The theory of entrepreneurial discovery allows economists to escape from the 'analytical box' in which 'choice' simply consists of computing a solution implicit in given data.

5. An entrepreneurial act of discovery consists in '...realising the existence of market value that has hitherto been overlooked'. Scope for entrepreneurial discovery occurs in a world of disequilibrium – which is quite different from the equilibrium world of mainstream economics where market outcomes are foreordained.

6. Entrepreneurial discovery explains why one price tends to prevail in a market. Though new causes of price differences continually appear, entrepreneurs exploit the resulting profit opportunities and produce a tendency towards a single price.

7. Only with the introduction of entrepreneurship is it possible to appreciate how markets work. Without entrepreneurship, there would be no market co-ordination.

8. So-called 'imperfections' of competition are often '...crucial elements in the market process of discovery and correction of earlier entrepreneurial errors'.

9. Advertising expenditures, for example, are means of alerting consumers to 'what they do not know that they do not know'. Anti-trust laws may hamper market processes and prevent competitive entry to markets.

10. Entrepreneurial profit, far from generating injustice, is a 'created gain'. It is not '...sliced from a pre-existing pie...it is a portion which has been created in the very act of grasping it'.

The Institute of Economic Affairs

2 Lord North Street, Westminster, London SW1P 3LB
Telephone: 0171 799 3745 Facsimile: 0171 799 2137
E-mail: iea@iea.org.uk Internet: http://www.iea.org.uk   ISBN 0-255 36404-0

£8.00